THE
NAKED
TRADER'S
BOOK
OF
TRADING
STRATEGIES

THE
NAKED
TRADER'S
BOOK
OF
TRADING
STRATEGIES

Proven ways to make
money investing in
the stock market

Harriman
House

HARRIMAN HOUSE LTD

3 Viceroy Court

Bedford Road

Petersfield

Hampshire

GU32 3LJ

GREAT BRITAIN

Tel: +44 (0)1730 233870

Email: enquiries@harriman-house.com

Website: harriman.house

First published in 2023.

Paperback ISBN: 978-0-85719-978-2

eBook ISBN: 978-0-85719-979-9

British Library Cataloguing in Publication Data

A CIP catalogue record for this book can be obtained from the British Library.

CONTENTS

THE END   237

INTRODUCTION
A Big Box
of Ideas

Welcome to *The Naked Trader's Book of Trading Strategies* – a big box of ideas for traders who want to add some money-making strategies to their arsenal.

A little bit about you

I guess around about now you might be wondering…

Is this book for me?

I hope so! It is not for total beginners: you need to be up and running with the basics, or to have read the latest edition of *The Naked Trader* first. But if you've bought this as a total beginner, don't worry. Just keep it by you while you learn the basics, then when you know what you're doing you'll be able to hit the ground running.

I don't expect you to have loads of trading experience either way. I imagine you know how to buy and sell shares and you've been doing it for a bit. But maybe you've been doing the same thing and it's not working anymore. Perhaps Covid wrecked your trading. Or post-pandemic market ups and downs have knocked your confidence.

Whatever it is, you need new ideas to try.

This book is here for you – including strategies to cope with hard events.

While this book is not for complete novices, don't be scared that it's going to be hugely advanced. I'm *not* going to write gobbledegook about technical strategies and all that. My *Naked Trader* books are all in plain English, and I tell it like it is. Because here's a little secret:

You don't actually need complexity to make money in the markets.

My strategies aren't complicated or scary. They're logical and easy to understand. And they work.

This book arms you with a ton of different strategies you can use in different market conditions. There's no need to gamble your way out of losses or become undisciplined. What you need are ideas that make money. And all of the ideas in this book have done just that for me, repeatedly.

How to use this book

This book is split into a few parts: the **Foundations** (quick but important), the **Strategies** (lots of them), and the **End** (all good things must come to one).

Do read the Foundations first. After that, feel free to dip in and out of the Strategies at will. You can read them from cover to cover, but they are in no particular order. Please do jump around if you like. Hate the sound of one? That's fine. You'll hopefully love the one after.

The point of this is deliberate: I like trading ideas that are simple and common-sense. If something takes forever to explain, I'm afraid I don't think it's likely to make you money.

Some trading strategies and systems are so elaborate it's like steadily ascending a skyscraper, and if you skip one chapter the whole edifice collapses. There's none of that here.

In my experience, you simply don't need it.

What if I'm not in the UK? Are there any strategies for international markets?

My previous books were largely for the UK market because I went into tons of detail on setting up your (UK) accounts and stuff like that. **This book should be helpful for any trader anywhere in the world.**

I do mention ISAs and SIPPs and spread betting a few times in this book (UK-specific trading accounts), but if you're not in the UK you can still use my methods to trade successfully – and indeed often find very similar accounts or tax wrappers in your home country.

When you come across that stuff, don't worry – just remember it's all about trading tax-free (where possible). You can use the underlying techniques in taxable accounts. Or in your country's version of tax-free accounts. And so on.

My examples are generally for the UK markets, but UK companies (especially on the FTSE 100) are highly international. If you're up and running in your trading, you should have no problem adapting my strategies to the particulars of the companies, indices and markets wherever you are.

Finding what works for you

It there's one big thing I've learned from 23 years of full-time trading and 17 years of talking to thousands of investors at seminars it's that traders hate changing. We get stuck in our ways. Even when it stops working. New strategies feel scary. But *every* trader needs an injection of new ideas from time to time.

You don't need to rush out and implement every one, of course. This book is designed to provide a large supply of inspirations, but you can just pick and mix and see how you go. And go *slowly*. It's all about finding what works for you.

Not every idea is for every trader. We all have different temperaments and portfolios. You might bounce off some of the ideas here. That's OK. But I hope you'll find a good number that you can add to whatever you do. Even one strategy that makes you money should be worth the £250 I'm assuming you've had to pay for this book with inflation as it is at the time of writing.

A few might also *save* you money. Most of the strategies are about what to do. But some talk about what *not* to do. Often, doing nothing – or simply avoiding something – can make you more money than all the action in the world. Trading is funny like that.

An active – but relaxed – way of trading

The only kinds of trader who will be out of luck here are: day-traders, technical analysts, forex and commodities obsessives, and anyone who thinks they can make millions in a few afternoons.

I'm a trader, but I'm interested in making longer-term money because that's the most reliable way of doing it. I'm kind of an investor in a way, just not one of those crusty ones who never checks their portfolio more than once a year (though that may be sensible for people with a different and less active approach to mine). I take action regularly. But I don't jump in and out all the time. I use charts, but in a simple and common-sense way. I can't stand bollocks. If you want bollocks, this book is not for you.

But if you want some strategies to make money, with patience, over time, then it definitely is!

The strategies in this book very much continue my relaxed 'tea-and-toast' trading style from *The Naked Trader*. These are strategies you can deploy quickly and simply, allowing you to get back to the real business of life: drinking Yorkshire tea with hot buttered toast.

There's no all-day sitting at your computer. It's disciplined, but relaxed. You can spend much more time loafing on the sofa instead.

Best of luck! Remember: the market is crazy. I hope this book helps you through some of the craziness.

Cheers,

Robbie

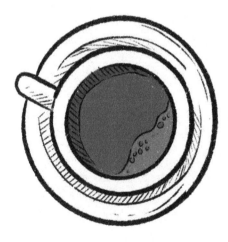

THE
FOUNDATIONS

The bare necessities

As I said in the introduction, this book is not for absolute beginners. But you don't have to be hugely experienced either. Rather than spend ages re-capping or qualifying what I have to say in the strategies that follow, I thought it might be helpful to share a quick summary of my trading methodology and what I expect of companies.

> All of this thinking goes into every strategy that follows. It's The Naked Basics. Or, if you like, the bare necessities. Please don't think any of these strategies are designed to let me (or you) skip them. The strategies rely on them (with some exceptions, which I will mention at the time).

Strategies are ways of putting the odds a little in your favour, or of finding effective angles of approach, or of surfacing new trade ideas – not shortcuts past the essentials.

You may have evolved your own set of essentials that have done you right. Please don't think I'm saying my way is the only way, or that you can't use my strategies without my basics. I just want to be upfront about the background work and thought that goes into every trade.

You might be able to swap bits of the below, or add to them, with your own stuff that works for you. That's fine!

1. **I check company reports and news** for good, bad and neutral news, using ADVFN.com's ability to highlight phrases (ADVFN. com > News > Highlight Phrases). I go into this in more detail in *The Naked Trader*, but you can probably work it out on your own using the site. Basically this helps me make a quick initial judgement – any company with lots of positive phrases ('exceeding expectations', 'favourable', 'profit up', 'transformational', etc.) is worth a closer look. Any with terrible ones ('below expectations', 'difficult', 'unpredictable', 'challenging', 'tough') is binned. You begin to get a good feel for key phrases over time. Companies love obscuring jargon. This breaks through that.

2. **I check the net debt.** This is a company's debt minus its cash and therefore really the most accurate way of seeing exactly how much it owes. Anything with a net debt more than three times the full-year pre-tax profit, I don't touch. It's too risky for me; I have seen too many companies like that go bust. Net cash is very good, by contrast.

3. **I check some key facts.** Market cap: if it's below £20m, or the amount I can trade is below £2,000, it's too illiquid and dangerous. Likewise, if it's actually currently losing money, no thanks. If the spread – the difference between the buy and sell price – is more than 5%, again, no thank you. If it's in oil or energy, ditto. And if Stockopedia has labelled it 'earnings manipulation risk' or a 'sucker stock', goodbye.

4. **Rising dividends are next.** They're a key good sign. If they're being cut or collapsing without some exceptional reason, I'm worried.

5. **Then I check the chart for the last year.** I really don't have any time for technical weirdness, as said. Maybe I'm missing out, but I have my methods and they've worked for me. Here, I'd like the company to be trending upwards. (Or, if I'm fishing for a

down-and-out stock, I want the early signs of a recovery after a
trend downwards.)

6. **I check the company isn't about to issue a report.** Even
if everything currently looks great, is there something that
could blindside my trade? And I check if there have been any
recent institutional buying or directors' dealings. I am especially
interested in the proportion of shares a director is buying
compared to how much they currently owe. It's a decent measure
of their belief in their firm.

7. **The price-earnings or PE ratio now gets a glance.** They're
pretty abstract, but can be useful for comparing companies with
others – they show you how the market is valuing companies
relative to each other. A PE of 12, say, in a sector averaging 21
means a company could be undervalued.

8. Finally, the **billionaire test.** I pretend I am a billionaire and
thinking not simply about sticking on a few grand in a trade, but
actually buying the particular company outright. I'd only do that,
of course, if it would make me my money back, and plenty more.
I have to know how much it's making, and how much it would
cost me to get that money, and if it wouldn't make Billionaire
Me interested, then Trader Me is out too.

When trading, I always use **stop-losses**. I tend to base these on
where a share found support previously. Sometimes I use what I
call a **Get Out Quick** – that is, I will quit a trade if it goes against
me very rapidly. E.g., I bought something but then only see sellers
and a big downwards pressure on the share price.

I'll list the stop-losses for tons of trading examples throughout the
book so you get a really good feel for how I calculate them.

Indeed there are loads and loads of real-life trading examples in the
pages that follow, illustrating all of the above research in action – as
well as the strategies to come. Most of these are now closed at a
profit. Some are still open at the time of writing (and I'll flag those).

If you want to catch up on how any trades have gone since I wrote this, just head to nakedtrader.co.uk and click on **Trades**.

Now it's time to quickly cover planning...

I love it when a plan comes together

It amazes me when traders don't plan their trades properly. Especially ones that have been doing this for a while.

As you've bought this book, you must be an upstanding citizen, so I'm sure you plan all your trades. But maybe you've let things slip and stopped using plans for a bit, or are no longer doing them so thoroughly. It's easy to believe our own hype, or trust our own instincts or experience.

But all of the world's highest performing traders with decades-long careers still plan all their trades. It helps you avoid lazy thinking, or trading for reasons other than a solid expectation of profit. It means you never find yourself in a position where you have an open trade but have to later ask yourself: "What did I actually want from this trade?" Or "What am I going to do if this goes wrong?"

Or: "This has gone wrong. Help!"

If you've gone back to not making plans with your trades, it is time to re-start!

You've decided to buy something. You did all the research, you think it's a great time to buy, everything looks good. Before you press that buy button you *must* have a plan and stick to it.

Once you have that plan, write it down, put it in your spreadsheet or notes app or whatever you use. Refer back to it throughout the lifetime of the trade – and, even better, when making plans for future trades. Remember: written records lead to outperformance over time.

Here's what I mean by a plan:

1. **What** I want from this trade and **when**. (A quick profit? Trading a range? A medium-term idea? A long-term tuckaway?)

2. **Why** the share price will move the way I expect it to.

3. The **current share price** and my **sell** targets (for some or all of the holding).

4. **How many** shares I am buying.

5. My **stop-loss**. (More on this in the next chapter.)

You can set up alerts on many trading platforms to let you know if your trade is going down or up and hitting certain specific levels. Take your planned action when that happens. You can also automate stops. A very good idea!

I don't think a target price should be set in stone like a stop. It should be more of a prompt to ask yourself: do I take some profit or not? Your alert will remind you to re-consider your stance on the trade at a higher price.

You might want to add the date of the next company results or statement to your plan too. This will help if you'll want to sell down a high-performing holding before good news (see **Sell before results** strategy). Or if a company is nearing your stop and more bad news is probably on the way – you might as well quit early and save some dosh before the company comes out with an inevitable profit warning.

If you're an advanced trader who knows all about Level 2, a share hitting these alerts is a good time to check that. (Don't worry if that's not you.)

The most important part of your plan is the stop-loss. No question at all. Activate it when hit. It's a rule!

But how do you know where to set it? That's the next chapter.

Top of the stops

I'm sure some of you have used stop-losses – but some of you won't have.

"Stops are for wimps," some say. And sometimes they just don't work well. You get spiked out and the share rises and you go: "That is *it* with stops."

But when the market is going down, you'll be very grateful.

If you don't use them, the problem is you may never sell a stinker – and it will keep on going down… and down… and the more it goes down, the less chance there is of taking the loss. You get emotional and caught up with the share.

Setting stops gets over this psychological hurdle. And you feel much better when the stinker has gone!

Look at these charts of some popular shares bought by investors. See how a stop-loss at almost any point would have got them safely out before worse!

Never ever move your stop down once you've decided where it should be. You can move it *up* should your share do well. There's no better feeling than moving a stop into break-even. At that point, you can't lose.

Boohoo indeed

Aston Martin – a car crash in slow motion

Or you can use a trailing stop-loss as discussed in depth in *The Naked Trader*, which kind of achieves the same thing automatically.

Most brokers will execute stops for you, and even set an alert so your email or phone will ping to let you know a stop is about to get hit.

It's all very well talking about putting in a stop but where?

Well, it's true, you really don't want to be spiked out on a quick move down. And you really can be. But you have to have some protection in place.

> I don't use percentages for stop-losses. I prefer to look at where the share has found support in the past, and set it a little below that.

Best thing is an example or two.

I bought **ME Group** at around 75p in June 2022 as it broke up, and set a stop at 66, just under where you can see it found support at 68 back in May. I always add extra to take spreads into account. As the share then rose to 100p, I could raise the stop up to 85p.

ME Group stop-loss

In July 2022, on buying **Ricardo** at 392, you can see the share didn't want to go below 340p in May – but given the spread on this share could go as wide as 10p, I set the stop at 330p. However, I'd also consider getting out quicker than that if it obviously started to tumble and Level 2 looked bad.

Ricardo stop-loss

On buying **Concurrent** in July 2022 at 77p, you can clearly see the shares found support twice at 70p in the previous two months. So I put my stop a little below that at 67p, again to account for any spread widening.

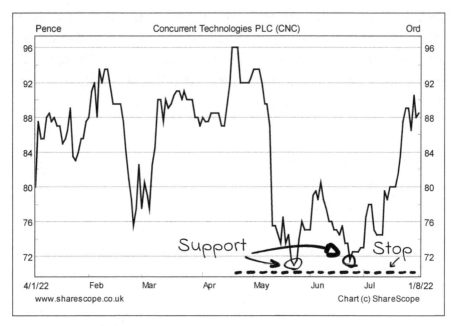

Pence — Concurrent Technologies PLC (CNC) — Ord

www.sharescope.co.uk — Chart (c) ShareScope

Concurrent stop-loss

It's important to take into account the usual spread of a share. For small caps, stops need to be a bit wider to account for this. But for FTSE 250 or 100 shares you can set your stops a little closer as the spreads are often minimal, especially on the 100.

Something very important to take into account with stops is noting when a share goes ex dividend, especially if it pays out a big dividend. From start of play on ex-dividend day, the shares normally start lower by the amount of the dividend – sometimes a little more, as the unwary get their stops hit.

Remember you get the dividend as cash in your account at a later date – but if your stop is within the likely fall, you'll get stopped out first thing. **Beware!**

Sadly, if there is a profit warning on a share overnight a stop *won't* save you. You'll be taken out early doors at a much worse price than your stop. Some brokers allow you to state a level where you don't want to be stopped out should a share start the day significantly lower (e.g. 40%).

If you're buying into a share that's going straight up – i.e. there is no support to see on a chart – try placing a stop at 10–15% below the buy price, depending on how keen you are to hold the share. Whatever happens, never let anything go more than 25% lower without cutting it.

The only place where your stop can be guaranteed is with spread bets.

I generally look at stops as an insurance policy against having bought a stinker or something at the wrong time. It takes me out unemotionally.

If you feel you made a mistake on a share and it starts tumbling right away, you don't have to wait for your stop. You could get out quick and take your medicine more rapidly! These are closer than stops and a manual thing, for when you're watching your trade closely at the start.

Overall, stops have saved me a fortune! Most recently when I traded broadcaster **ITV**, where I got stopped out for a loss at 100p after a statement that wasn't well received by the market. Later that week the shares were *82p!*

I really urge you to use stops. I reckon if people had used stops over the last couple of years on tanking shares, they'd have saved millions and millions in losses. There is plenty of evidence on forums of people losing lots by not using them.

So, stop! Use stops.

Start right now.

And now it's onto the strategies...

THE
STRATEGIES

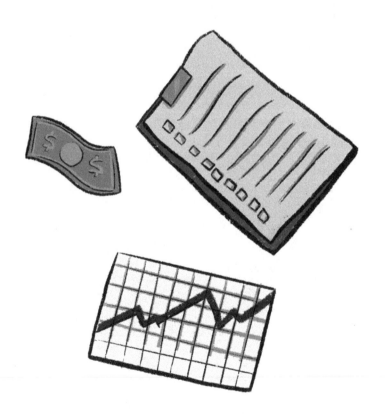

Trade the news

Keeping an eye on what's happening in the news has always been a bit of a strategy for me. When Covid hit in early 2020, I wondered: what companies might actually benefit from everyone being forced to stay at home?

An idea came about from a chat with the missus. People stuck at home = bored people. And people sitting around all day looking at their house. So of course it won't be long before they decide to get some DIY done.

"Where will people get their DIY stuff from?" I asked.

"B&Q," said the missus.

It didn't take much research to discover that B&Q and a number of other DIY and building brands were owned by a firm called **Kingfisher**. And their shares were down, along with basically every other company at this time.

My idea was simply to buy Kingfisher shares while everyone else was busy buying their DIY wares. The shares were trading at 150p on 28 April 2020 when I enacted the following plan.

The plan – Kingfisher

- Buy price: 150p
- Target: 200p? 250p? (Let's see. This was one to watch closely, alongside the news.)
- Stop-loss: 130p

What happened next

After I put my trade on, the shares started to rise. And… didn't stop. By July Kingfisher put out a statement saying they were soaring. Why? You guessed it: because of the popularity of DIY.

I started to add a few more as the share price rose. By September 2020 the shares were over 300p. I had doubled my money.

Once a trade doubles I tend to think you should at least take *some* money off the table. However, on this occasion I just sold everything. I thought: it isn't a tech share that might double again. It's only a retailer. Also, people were going back to work – perhaps the DIY boom was reaching its peak.

I sold the shares for 304p at the back end of October 2020 for a profit of £7,690.

If I had held on for a few months more, I would have seen the shares hit 350p in 2021. In retrospect, it might have been better to wait. However, the shares fell before then – it was a bumpy ride.

All in all, I am totally happy with the trade.

Kingfisher – a DIY-lightful trade

Lessons learned

- Keep an eye on the news. When big things happen, they can affect prices.

- There is nothing wrong with banking a profit even if a share goes a little higher afterwards. You should always think: I am happy with part of a ride, I'm unlikely to always find the top or bottom of everything.

- You can get ideas from people you know. Of course, that's just the start of your research.

Talk to the staff

It is amazing how much intelligence you can gather on a potential share purchase just by talking to a company's staff as a customer.

If you are using a listed company's services or products, ask staff how busy they have been. Chat with them; try and find out what's going on.

And ask other customers, too. How was their experience? Come to that, how was yours? (Maybe don't ask yourself this out loud on the shop floor.)

I found **Spire Healthcare**, a chain of independent hospitals, when I was booked into one of their places for an injection. I was trundled into a lovely upmarket cubicle and immediately got chatting to the staff.

"We are just so busy," they said. "We need all the staff we can get at the moment. There's no sign of it stopping."

On the way out, I needed a push in a chair, and chatted to the porter. He agreed: "Rushed off my feet," he said. "It has never been this busy!"

As soon as I got home I had a quick check of Spire Healthcare's financials. No real red flags appeared. Armed with my knowledge of increased demand for their services, I bought some shares at 137p just before Christmas 2020.

The plan – Spire Healthcare

- Buy price: 137p
- Target: 220p
- Stop-loss: 115p

What happened next

By early 2021 the shares had begun to rise. Then a bit of luck: there was a bid for Spire from another healthcare group in June 2021. The shares leapt higher as a result.

Given the excellent rise in the price, I sold in June 2021 for 251p – banking around a £7,000 profit.

As things turned out that was a good move: eventually the bid fell through and the shares fell a bit (though not that much).

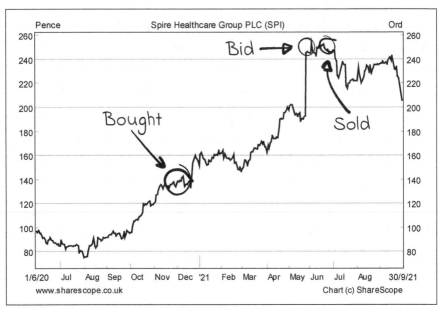

Spire Healthcare – in-spireing!

Another one!

It was a similar story with **Watches of Switzerland**.

My wife had set her heart on a Rolex for our 20th wedding anniversary (all together now: *ahhhhh....*). I was never a watch person myself, with only four of the same £5 timepiece set to different times. (Europe, US, Middle East and the UK – if I'm going somewhere, all I need to do is switch watches.)

We went along to a branch of Watches of Switzerland. What an eye opener! It was incredibly busy. The staff were run off their feet. The lady serving us confirmed things had never been that hectic. She said the flash watches market had really taken off. Prices of Rolexes (Rolexi?) were heading up, as were those of pretty much every other smart brand.

Apparently not only did these watches hold their value but it was even possible to make a profit on your second-hand fancy timepiece. A whole new world to me.

After parting with an eye-watering amount for the wife's watch, I couldn't wait to get home to check out the company's fundamentals.

Reading through the company's statements I could see growth was definitely there and that they were planning to conquer the US by opening up a number of new shops. I learned that even in a recession the prices of these watches were likely to go higher.

Profit forecasts for the company were excellent, with profits expected to rise substantially. The only thing I could see that could be a ticking time bomb was the high net debt. But debt levels were within my usual parameters – less than 3× net debt to forecast profits.

Also, its net fixed assets were higher than the debt – all looked OK. And I guess it would be hard to go bust with all those expensive watches sitting there.

The plan – Watches of Switzerland

- Buy price: 950p (Sept 2021), 1050p (October 2021)
- Target: 1250p
- Stop-loss: 75p below entry prices

I bought two lots of shares, one lot for 950p at the end of September 2021 and some more in mid-October for around 950p then 1050p. Stops were 75p lower than the entry prices.

What happened next

Shares rose a lot, up to 1500p by November 2021.

I wasn't sure whether to take profits so I used a trailing stop, which got me out at 1344 and 1420 respectively, for an overall profit of just under £4,000.

Watches of Switzerland – the kind of tick-tock I can understand

Lessons learned

- Always keep your eyes open when you are out and about. And get chatting. You never know what financial intelligence you might pick up.

- Talking to the staff – or customers – is only the starting point. Research comes next. Never buy just because of something people tell you. You have to run the numbers.

- This strategy can also help you pick up on when companies aren't doing well – which gives you the potential of going short.

Trade the phrase 'ahead of expectations'

If there's one phrase that really jumps out at me when I see a trading statement, it's when a company is described as performing 'ahead of expectations'. The exact wording can vary, of course, but so long as it's along these lines, I'm interested.

If there's one phrase that's even better, it's '*substantially* ahead of expectations'.

Oh yes!

These simple words on a trading statement grab my attention because they mean something is going very right for the company involved, and it's likely to be in a good place for the foreseeable future.

If you're already holding a share that is performing 'ahead of expectations' then you can probably push it into a longer-term hold category. Now is the time to sit back and do nothing (perhaps just put the kettle on).

Otherwise you can often buy in knowing that results are likely to be decent for a while. Chances are good that the next few statements will show the share price going up. At the very least you'll be invested in a share that isn't likely to fall substantially.

The best way to find these 'ahead of expectations'-type companies is to run through daily market statements when they appear, just after 7am. Don't expect to get much out of this strategy if you prefer a lie-in of a morning!

I use the free website investegate.co.uk to access these reports.

Even though you might be tempted to buy straight away when you spot a statement like this, bear in mind that some shareholders will want to take profits after such good news. It can be worth waiting a little before snapping up the shares they sell.

Bloomsbury, the UK publisher of the *Harry Potter* books, was listed as performing "materially ahead of market expectations" in its statement of 26 January 2022. By the end of March 2022 this had improved to "materially ahead of upgraded expectations".

I bought both times on the strength of these statements.

In October 2022, an 'ahead of' trading statement was released by a company I hadn't come across before in October 2022 – online bathroom retailer, **Victorian Plumbing**. I just happened to notice it when news statements were coming out on 6 October 2022.

There I was, lying in bed with no plans to do much that day, when I stumbled across a very strong statement. There were lots of phrases I like to see, including "ahead of market consensus". And, what's that? £43m in net cash! Big tick! Revenue up 78% compared to pre-Covid! Another tick: all online, no massive chain of expensive shops to pay for…

I leapt out of bed pronto, only 15 mins till market open. (Despite this, tea and toast comes before money at all times so I did lose a vital ten minutes.)

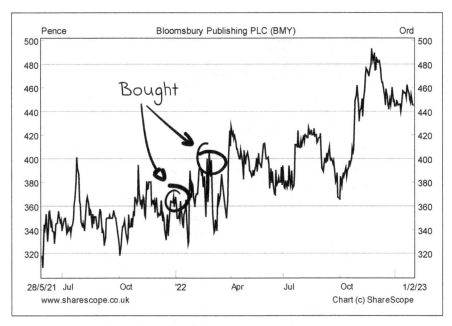

Bloomsbury – blooming marvellous

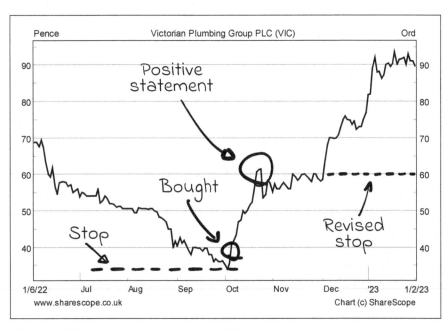

Victorian Plumbing – bathing in profit

I checked all the fundamentals. Shares had been over 300p just a few months previously. Now they were at 39p on a tiny PE of just 8. With a mountain of cash and a very decent results statement likely due soon, it felt like a no-brainer.

I went in after I'd finished my Yorkshire Gold and bought a couple of times at 39p. My stop was at 34p, and no idea on a target! I just wanted in. This one was probably one of the easiest buying decisions I've ever had to make.

Shares gradually climbed to 75p. I've stayed in, running the profits and moving the stop up to 60p. My plan now is to keep the stop 15p behind the peak price, given it can get volatile.

Lessons learned

- It's better to be in shares exceeding expectations than those issuing profit warnings.

- You can't go far wrong by having some shares of companies that consistently come up with 'ahead of...' statements in your portfolio.

- Sometimes you may need to move fast if a report looks especially good and a share price hasn't moved a lot higher prior to the report. Other times if a share price has already gone a lot higher there might be some profit taking even on an 'ahead of', and you might want to wait for the profit-takers to finish, er, taking profits before moving in.

- The time to take profits on these shares is when a new statement isn't as bullish as recent ones.

- One variation on this strategy would be to buy a small amount of the shares when you see a strong statement and then add some more a day or a week later (once other shareholders have taken profits).

Use your industry knowledge

I have noticed a real blind spot from talking to traders and investors over the years. Many of them have detailed and first-hand knowledge of a particular industry (their current or past day-job, perhaps, or maybe just the financial industry itself). But they don't use that knowledge to trade shares in said industries.

Note! If you work for a company in a particular sector then you have priceless knowledge. It amazes me that people don't think about using that knowledge to buy or short shares in their industry.

Some real-life examples:

- I once met an airline pilot who had *massive* knowledge of the state of his and other airlines, but wasn't trading any of them. They were in dire straits at the time, and he knew it, and could have shorted them and made tons. He hadn't even considered it.

- I once spoke with a film producer who had countless industry contacts but who wasn't trading film facility companies or broadcasters.

- I once chatted with someone who had extensive knowledge of the building trade but wasn't getting involved with builders' shares. He actually said to me: "Everyone reckons Morgan Sindall is the best in the industry and they're doing really well." Did he have any shares? "No, I never thought about it!" he replied. When we spoke the shares were 1300p, a few months later they were 2500p!

- I once talked to someone in publishing. He said everyone was buying physical books; Kindles were dead. Yet... he hadn't thought about buying a listed publisher.

What industry are you in? Or, who do you know that works in a particular industry or area?

You may, for example, work in a pub and know sales are picking up. If they are picking up for you, it's probably the same elsewhere – and worth looking at listed companies in the hospitality sector.

Hang on, isn't this illegal insider trading?

Not at all: **insider trading is only when you have definite knowledge that the market doesn't know about yet which could substantially alter a company's share price**.

Let's say you know a company is about to be taken over. Or a friend says: "Don't tell anyone, we just won a massive contract." Trading shares in these companies because of this information would be insider dealing as you now know specific info which will soon affect the share prices once the market is told.

It *isn't* insider dealing if you don't have specific info unknown to the market as a whole.

So…

- What industry do you have knowledge of?
- What industry do friends have knowledge of?
- What listed companies are in a similar industry?
- Can you take advantage of knowing how well or not that industry is faring?

Sometimes it can be easy! I happened to go to a couple of shopping areas while the Mrs had her nails done. Sitting outside a **Card Factory** and a **Joules** store, both hardly saw a customer buy anything at a peak time.

"Hmm," I thought, "that's not good." I went home, checked them out, and shorted both companies.

I ended up shorting Joules in February 2022 at 70p and took profits of £2,300 at 23p in July 2022. I was worried the shares might go bust – and when that happens and you're short of a share it can take some time to get the money (the spread bet firm has to be sure it is definitely kaput). Joules did end up getting de-listed at 9p soon after I quit the trade, so if I had been a bit braver I would have made a little more.

Joules – from riches to rags

Card Factory ended as a nice profit of a grand, selling at 64p in May 2022 and buying back at 43p in October.

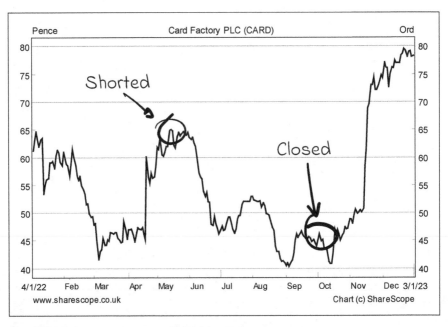

Card Factory – an open and shut trade

I walked away with handsome profits – having specialised with a little bit of knowledge!

Lessons learned

- You might have valuable industry information without knowing it. Think about what you know about an industry from first-hand experience, and use it to find similar companies that could be about to out (or under) perform.

- Ask friends and family too.

- Don't use specific information unavailable to the wider market which will soon alter a company's share price. That's insider trading.

Spot bid targets in hot sectors

I n 2021 a number of the companies whose shares I had bought received bids. In other words, some other businesses wanted to hoover them up. To do that, of course, you typically have to offer more than the current market price for the shares. So I had a very good time.

Even if a bid target isn't eventually bought, the process is also usually positive for the share price in the short term.

How do you find something that will get bid for?

I bet you'd love a definite answer like: "It's easy, press this button here, and hey presto! Here is a list of shares that will definitely get bid for."

But, as you've done some trading already, you'll know it's not that simple.

To find such shares, you really have to keep your eyes and ears open. This is where it's worth scanning the business pages of a decent paper like *The Times* or *FT*. You might read rumours or news about such-and-such a company being bid for. Your next step is to look at other companies in the same sector: once a sector is hot, other bids often arise.

The other question to ask is: do a lot of the companies in this sector pretty much do the same thing? If so, bigger companies might be interested in snapping them up as a quick and easy way to grow.

Computer game craziness

In 2020 I noticed the shares of all computer game companies were going higher. *The Times* picked up on this too. Some of it was because bored people working from home were playing computer games a lot more. So I did a comparison of listed games companies.

You can do this manually or you can cheat and do it on Stockopedia pretty quickly by selecting a share, scrolling down and clicking on the comparison tool:

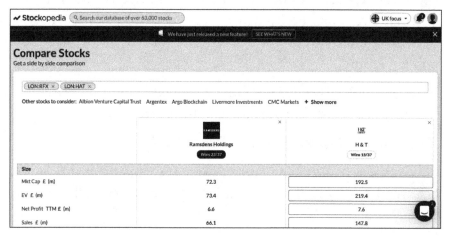

Comparing a share on Stockopedia

When I did this I noted that the games developer **Codemasters** had a much lower PE ratio than similar companies Team 17 and Frontier Developments. The PE or price-to-earnings ratio, as you'll know, simply means the number of years it will take for the earnings of a company to cover the share price. A lower one means a cheaper company compared to firms with higher ones.

I therefore went for Codemasters as the buy here.

The plan – Codemasters

- Buy price: 300p, 328p
- Target: 400p, 450p
- Stop-loss: 290p, 270p

What happened next

I picked up shares in May 2020 for 300p, then as it kept going up I kept buying more. I bought again at 328p in July and at just under 500p in November.

A bid was announced in December 2020 and indeed a bidding war started, but I sold all the shares because the share price had soared ahead of the bid price. Frankly I have no idea what happened after that, as I was happy selling at 654p just before Christmas for a profit of nearly £20,000.

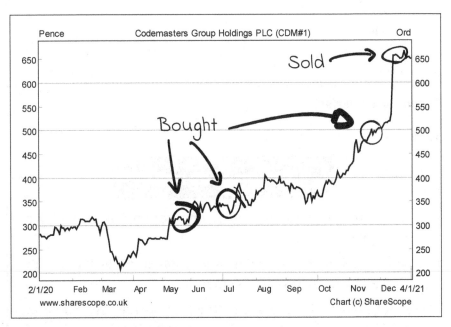

Codemasters – digital delights

But that is not the end of the story.

After the Codemasters bid I did another scan of games shares and found **Sumo,** which seemed to do pretty much the same as Codemasters. I bought some of their shares for 309p in December 2020 and held on, hoping for a bid there. Luckily for me a bid came in for Sumo in August 2021, and I sold for 490p, banking £1,800 on that trade.

Sumo – pixel perfect

Game on!

Lessons learned

- Keep an eye on the papers to find hot sectors where bids are likely.
- Always compare companies in a sector to make sure you're buying the most attractive company.
- A hot sector will often see multiple companies get bid for in a fairly short space of time. You can get several trades out of finding one.

Sell before results, buy back later

Something I've seen a lot more of lately is a very decent share getting sold off on results day and in the days after. This drives investors wild! "Why oh why?" they moan.

Their favourite share has been going up and they are very happy, indeed boasting to their friends about how much money they're making. Their friends probably roll their eyes, waiting for the company to do badly later in the year. Instead, the company results are great! The trader is vindicated! What a smarty-pants. But then the share price actually *tumbles*.

What?! How can such an amazing company be treated like that? Well, an old stock market cliché has stuck around for a reason: 'Buy the story, sell the news.'

The share price went up a lot because the good news was *expected*. Once the good news is out, traders say: "Well, OK, we got the positive results we anticipated, the shares have had a good run, time to take profits." Which of course makes the price go *down*.

Often profit-takers gather momentum, and shares carry on falling for a few days. But this painful reality isn't just something traders have to learn to live with. It presents an opportunity.

- If you are in a great share, it is way up and has been rising strongly, it can be a good strategy to sell some of your holding the day before and bank some profits.

- Or, take a chance, sell *all*, wait for the price drop and buy back a few days or weeks later – once the profit-takers are gone.

> I'm talking shares that have gone up maybe 20% before results. That kind of surge means part of the success of the company is baked into the share price. The actual results have to be way, way better than expected for the share price to carry on rising on results day.

You'll sometimes find a good news story will initially push the share price up. But then, traders will come in and bank their profits. Wait till they're done, and buy up.

If in doubt about selling a good one before results, go in and research it again. Has the rating now gone too high for your liking after a big rise? Perhaps it isn't the bargain it was when you initially bought it?

In which case a decision to bank profits might be an easy one.

Time for an example. In November 2022, shares in **Argentex** (an FX company) had risen strongly from 75p to 120p. The market knew the statement would be decent, hence the rise – but it would probably have to be *ultra* decent to rise more.

It would have been wise to bank some profits a day or two before the statement at near 120p. On 8 November – the day of the statement – the shares began to retreat on profit taking. Two days later, on 10 November, shares had retreated back to 95p. A great time to buy back or top up.

By the middle of the following week, shares were back up past 100p – and climbed again from there. A perfect example of *buy the rumours* and *sell on/before the news.* Then wait a bit for profit-takers to come, before buying back in.

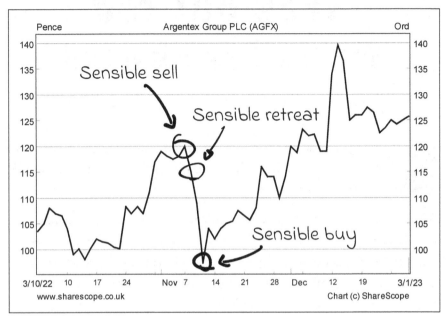

Argentex – crafty like a FX

Lessons learned

- Don't get mad about good shares getting sold off on good news. It's not random, nor does it mean a company is a dud. It's because of how the stock market works. It's all about expectations.

- If you're in a great share whose price has surged before results, think about selling some or all of your holding the day before results.

- Wait till profit-takers are done – a few days or weeks – then buy back in.

Seek out red flags for shorts

Shorting shares, as you'll know, means betting on them to go down. It's easy to do with a spread betting account in the UK. But it takes a mindset shift.

With a normal trade or investment, there's a limited downside (you can only lose 100% of your money) and unlimited upside (shares can, in theory, keep going up forever, and profits of 1,000% or more are not unheard of – e.g. if you held Apple from IPO, you've made nearly *70,000%*, well done Mr Money).

With shorting, the reverse is true.

> **NT Note!** When you short a share, *your downside is potentially unlimited*. So you have to be sensible and disciplined.

If I'm going to short a share, what do I want to see? Red flags, and lots of them.

Trainline is a good example of this in action. By mid-2020, this UK digital rail and coach ticket vendor had developed more or less all of the red flags I'd look for in a short. Every time I saw it mentioned in market news it was to add another red flag to its collection.

Three big ones in particular were especially red and flappy:

1. A massive market cap when weighed against likely profits. Even after big falls in early 2020 it was still valued at over £1bn, with

profits of £31m forecast for the year ahead. But it was making losses, with a net debt of £163m.

2. Directors and founders had been selling like crazy ever since the firm had been listed on the stock market in June 2019. Most worrying to me was CEO Claire Gilmartin selling off shares in a rush (maybe she had a train to catch). And these were not small numbers!

3. Gilmartin had sold off £15m almost as soon as she could after the IPO in 2019. She then sold another £3m worth in early 2020 (and would later sell another £400,000 in early 2021). KMR, a massive shareholder, also dumped tons of shares shortly after Trainline listed, as did other directors.

You get the picture. Trainline was overvalued. And it looked to me as if they knew it. Stockopedia summed it up well by grading Trainline as a "sucker stock". It wasn't long before they gave the company an all-time low rating of 5 out of 100.

Things looked increasingly bleak for Trainline shares.

All of this added up to a giant signal to get short in this share!

The plan – Trainline (short)

- Sell price: 520p
- Target: 450p
- Stop-loss: 570p

What happened next

I first started shorting Trainline in mid-2020 at around 520p. From there I kept selling as the share price went down.

I did take some profits on the way down. As it turned out, this was a mistake – because although there were some rallies (as you can see from the chart) the price generally kept on going down, so I generally kept adding to the short.

At the time of writing, I still had the short open. I think the company is only worth £500m at best.

Trainline – off the rails

To sum this one up, it might be one to present to Peter Jones from *Dragons' Den* (see **Be a Dragon** strategy). "Peter, would you like to offer me over a billion quid for my amazing ticketing company? We're making losses, have a big debt, and people are using trains less. Deal?!"

Lessons learned

- When you see loads of red flags, consider going short.
- Although there will be rallies in red flag shares, eventually shares like Trainline will hit the buffers (pun intended).
- I wish I had been braver and shorted more.

Buy bouncebacks

While Kingfisher (see **Trade the news** strategy) was all about what would do well during the Covid-19 pandemic, when the pandemic appeared to be waning I wondered which companies might benefit from a post-Covid bounceback.

In January 2022 we decided it was high time to get out of the UK for the first time in two years, and booked some flights with **easyJet**. We weren't the only ones to think about taking our first holiday in what felt like forever – we knew of other friends who had booked trips abroad for the summer even further in advance. Bookings would likely rise substantially as the summer holiday season approached.

This got me thinking about share prices in the travel industry. I don't ordinarily buy airlines because I find them impossible to value. There are too many factors to weigh up – the oil price, the value of airplanes and landing slots, debt, etc. I therefore didn't bother looking at fundamentals for this one and played it quite simply as a recovery play for beaten-down airlines.

Since the Covid-19 pandemic began, easyJet shares had fallen from 1600p to under 600p, which made sense. However, I felt sure that once countries opened up again flights would get back to somewhere near normal.

Sure, the shares were unlikely to take off all the way back to pre-Covid levels, but maybe they could recover to, say, halfway there?

The plan – easyJet

- Buy price: 518p
- Target: 1100p
- Stop-loss: 470p

I bought 1,000 shares at 518p on 21 December 2021, hoping to take a profit up near a tenner in time. I also decided that, should the shares start to rise nicely, I might average up and buy some more.

Working out where to get out was a bit harder given the shares were very volatile, sometimes up and down 30p in a day, depending on sentiment. I stuck a stop in at 470p and planned to gradually raise that under the price. I soon managed to raise the stop up to just over breakeven at 520p as the shares rose over 600p.

What happened next

easyJet shares kept on rising, but by February 2022 stories began to emerge that maybe all might not be so bright for airlines – with Russia invading Ukraine. I tightened the stop to 714p, close to the then-price, and was closed out for a profit of nearly £2,000.

easyJet – we have take-off

Another one!

I also decided to get some exposure to the holiday market and went for **Jet2com**, a fairly large, well-known and seemingly respected package holiday/plane company. Again I found this one very hard to value, so frankly I didn't try (except to note it had net cash of nearly £300m – nice).

The plan – Jet2com

- Buy price: 986p
- Target: 1500p
- Stop-loss: 900p

I bought 600 shares at 986p on the same day that I bought the easyJet shares. As with those, I targeted a decent rise, something in the region of 1500p, and again decided to average up if they went up.

I set the stop at 900p with (like easyJet) the idea of gradually raising the stop up under the price (but keeping a safe distance, as the shares were very volatile).

My feeling regarding both shares was that should any new variant of Covid-19 arrive which could disrupt the summer holidays, I would need to make a sharp exit.

What happened next

As with easyJet, when the war in Ukraine hit, shares began to tumble and a tightened stop-loss got hit at 1415p in mid-Feb for a profit of nearly £3,000.

Jet2com – wheels up

I got unlucky and lucky with these travel ideas.

Unlucky in that the Ukraine war began pushing back prices. But lucky in that I took note and pushed up the stops to take profits.

After that I decided to leave the travel market alone until the war finished and oil prices came back down. I have a note to myself to return to both easyJet and Jet2com once the war is (hopefully soon) resolved.

Lessons learned

- You can potentially relax some of your usual rigorous trading criteria when making a recovery play of companies truly beaten up by circumstances beyond their control which are finally turning around (though not the criteria that check if they're about to go bust!).

- However, use stop-losses and be careful – be mindful that you have less protection against things going against you.

- If you are in a good profit and the price starts to ease, consider pushing your stop close to the current price. That enables you to ride the price higher – but profits will get taken should the trade head south.

- If the conditions for your trade changes, perhaps just bank the profit.

Beware bandwagons

Everyone loves a bandwagon. And we've all experienced the fear of missing out. When everyone else is making money but us, it hurts. The urge to get aboard for even crazy stuff can be overwhelming – even when there are no profits and valuations are obviously bonkers.

This strategy is one of a few in the book about making money by *not* doing something. And that something you don't want to do is jumping aboard bandwagons of bullshit heading straight for a big ditch.

Here's how to make a ton of money by simply avoiding that.

Firstly, let's learn from some classic recent examples.

The US stock market trading platform **Robinhood** was one of the biggest bandwagons during Covid. It seemed like everyone wanted to be an at-home trader. And everyone wanted to do it on Robinhood (at least in the States). And everyone wanted to buy Robinhood on Robinhood, of course.

The firm debuted on the stock market at $38 per share in late July 2021, then surged to $70.39 less than a week later. As it happened, that was to be its all-time high.

Everyone seemed to wake up, and down it went.

At the time of writing it sits at $10 per share. It's been sitting there or thereabouts since February 2022.

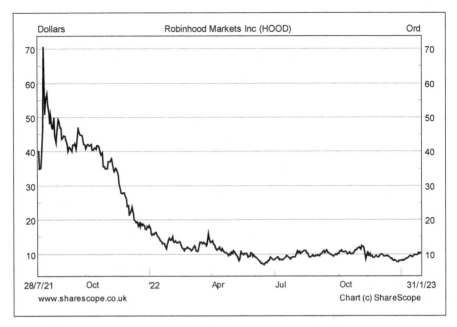

Robinhood – no merry men here

Perhaps an even more interesting example of a bandwagon to beware of was **GameStop**, the US video games retailer. 'Robinhood traders' bought this one, too, following in the footsteps of an online message board movement (which partly believed in the company, partly wanted to buy it for fun, and partly wanted to punish some hedge funds who had taken out extravagant short positions against it).

On 11 January 2021, the company's shares closed the day at $19.94. By 27 January they closed at an incredible *$347.51*. Less than a week later, on 4 February, they were down to $57.50. Unbelievable! The bandwagon was big news at the time, partly because much of the world was locked inside worrying about the Kent variant (remember that?).

If you tried to hop aboard it, unless you had exceptional luck and brilliant footwork, you basically landed on your arse.

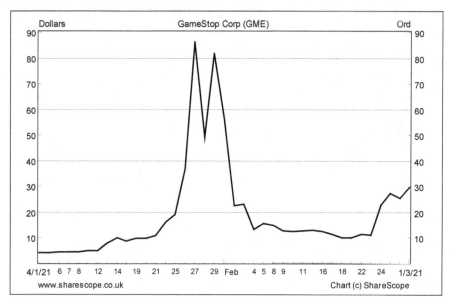

GameStop – bandwagon madness

Pie-in-the-sky thinking

In 2020 someone who worked at a company called Global persuaded me to start a podcast called *Naked Money*. The idea was that I would try to teach a young millennial how to buy and sell shares. I thought it sounded like a bit of fun.

Each episode, we would both bring a couple of shares, discuss them and buy one for a joint portfolio, then see how those shares performed.

A pattern soon emerged.

I would pick a share I felt a reasonable value could be put on; something with a dividend, in a growing market, that sort of thing. I'd talk about profits.

My lovely millennial mentee would always come up with a US tech share. He wouldn't mention figures at all, because he didn't really know what they were. He didn't care either. Nor did anyone else buying up US tech shares. It didn't matter because all tech shares were going up. Tech share? Just buy it!

"Yes, but it's valued at $80 billion, and it's making a loss. We'd be crazy to buy it!" I'd moan.

He'd say, "OK, but it has an amazing app that every teenager will soon have on their phone, and they'll make a fortune."

I'd say: "Maybe, but it's not proved, it's all pie in the sky…"

Every week would pretty much be the same. My boring share and his high-flying tech share.

In the end we ended up buying one or two of his. I felt like an out-of-touch teacher who'd been doing the same thing for years, with a new pupil who was showing me to be ancient and set in my ways.

"Roblox!" he said during one episode of the podcast. "That's my pick this week. Teenagers love it, it lets them socialise and play video games for free. Plus they can explore 3D interactivity and stuff."

"That's all well and good," I said, "but what about the numbers? It's valued at $70bn and is forecast to make a loss of nearly a billion."

"Yeah, but look at the price, it's going up!"

"Frankly," I replied, "this looks to be more like a load of *robollox*." (I think that may have got edited out of the podcast.) "I mean," I continued, "aren't there a lot of other companies in this space? Maybe it simply *won't* make a profit. There's no sign of any for $70bn."

This kind of conversation continued over the weeks.

"Coinbase!" said my millennial. "It's what everyone uses to buy bitcoin, just look at the share price!"

"But what if bitcoin is really bit*con*?" I asked. "What if things go wrong and people can't access their *bitcons*?"

He was desperate to get some bitcon action. After trying the "But Coinbase is forecast to make a loss for at least the next two years" routine, I gave in and we bought some. And some robollox.

I said, "OK, we'll get them, but if they tank we'll have to get out quickly."

In the end, most of our portfolio consisted of my 'boring' shares, simply because any of his that we bought ended up losing quickly – and my stop-losses (thankfully) got us out.

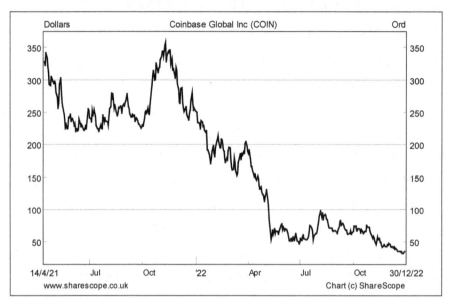

Coinbase – the future, once

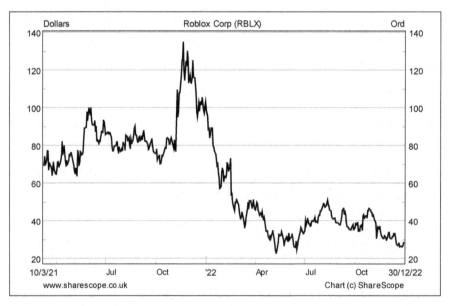

Roblox – if only it was boring

Lessons learned

- Don't get caught up by hype. If a sector is hot, that can be a good reason to get interested. Maybe you'll find bid targets, for instance (see **Spot bid targets** strategy). But hype alone won't last for long and cannot be the basis for a sound trade.

- Bonkers is bonkers, even if loads of people are really excited by it all of a sudden. Cultivate a world-weary scepticism about such stories. If a surging stock is on the nightly news on every channel, don't bloody buy it!

- Always ask: what do the numbers say?

- Stories of people making fortunes overnight drive lots of the worst bandwagons. Some people made millions on GameStop, and those stories brought countless people into the trade. The BBC interviewed people in the UK who'd got in on it for crying out loud! But it's really no more helpful to your trading to dwell on that than learning that someone won the Euromillions last night.

- You can make millions of profits over the long term in trading with low risk (that's what I've done). Trying to make millions overnight with *high* risk is a very good way to blow up your trading account and actually miss out on those millions – forever.

Don't get emotional!

This is another 'don't' strategy. You really can make thousands of pounds by *not* getting emotional. Indeed you can build an entire career in the markets that way!

I bet you skip this one, thinking "Pah – this is some psychological BS. What does Burns know about psychology? No qualifications or anything. Went to some crappy journalism college after getting an E in History. Hopeless!"

True, but I have met an awful lot of traders over the years and it is one thing I really know about from 'real life'.

Getting emotional is fatal for traders. I have heard the stories of countless traders who blew up because of it. It won't have been their only mistake, of course – but getting emotional will often be at the heart of things.

They got angry about a share going against them, closed the trade and immediately placed a short – only for the company to bounce and bite them twice.

Or they got upset about taking profits too early, bought back in big time without running the numbers again and seeing if the price really had further to go – and it turned out it didn't.

They put trades on because they're feeling down and want a buzz, not because their research indicates it makes sense. Or they can't bear to lose, and snatch at wins before they're fully developed. On and on it goes.

You see this emotion on discussion forums all the time. I'll always remember the company **Unbound**. (I know, sounds like an S&M company, but in fact it used to be a private equity and investment trust firm, before recently converting to... footwear.)

People ranted and raved and blamed all kinds of things for their losses as the share cratered from 120p to 12p throughout the course of 2021 and 2022.

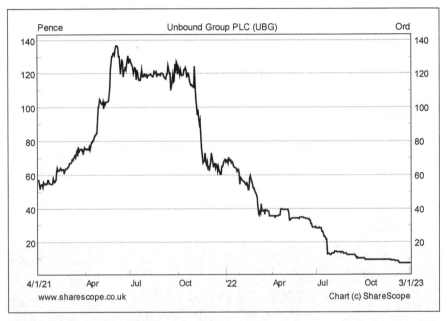

Unbound – traders bound by emotion

The management sucked, they were putting out false statements, they ranted. *The company didn't warn enough about deteriorating circumstances,* they raved. *But it looked so cheap,* claimed some more. And on and on.

What really happened was people got emotional. They watched the share price go down most days and didn't do anything. They couldn't bring themselves to sell it. Worse, they bought more as it went lower.

If they weren't that emotional they could have seen the many warnings coming from the company regarding difficult circumstances. They could easily have set stop-losses too.

I never go on these message boards, but couldn't help myself this time. Here's what I wrote.

> "I was interested to read today's comments on Unbound. But no one has mentioned the obvious: use stops. Especially in a down market.

> "Any stop put in at any point would have taken you out of Unbound with small losses. Get rid of losers. Sigh, swear, admit it was a dud, sell. If you wanted to you could wait and buy back lower later on. But cut the loss instead of averaging down.

> "There seems a lot of confirmation bias around and emotional energy used up. Don't go wasting your precious time, as the Spice Girls once said."

Taking a loss is the hardest thing because it confirms you made a mistake. No one likes coming face to face with that. But it's only by doing so that you can actually avoid a bigger and more deadly mistake that will overtake your entire trading career.

Of the many thousands of struggling traders I have met over the years, holding onto losers is the biggest reason for their inability to make money.

Remember, shares are just bits of companies. They don't care about you. They don't even know you exist. Treat them accordingly. And watch for signs of getting emotional in your trading. If you find yourself:

- checking the price constantly

- monitoring forums for positive comments

- thinking about a company outside trading hours or late at night

- cursing yourself for getting it wrong

- reassuring yourself it's only a loss on paper and will come back

- claiming you haven't made a mistake despite the trade going against you

- contemplating writing a letter to the CEO

then you should quit the share, wipe it from your screen, stop reading forum comments about it, and move on. There are plenty more profitable trades out there waiting for you.

Bloody sell it!

Lessons learned

- Emotions lead to bad trading decisions – always.

- Monitor yourself for signs of emotion taking hold.

- Use stop-losses to get out of shares unemotionally. (Use a written planning process to get *into* them unemotionally.)

- Acknowledging you made a mistake by selling a share hurts. But don't beat yourself up. It's a good thing. People who can sell losers can become long-term winners. Those who don't or can't, never do.

- If a trading thesis definitely (unemotionally) still makes sense to you, you can wait and buy back lower later on. But *cut the loss* instead of averaging down.

Dash for (net) cash!

Cash is unfashionable these days. Sometimes you can't even get a cup of coffee with a £5 note. "Cards only, please."

Well, stuff you. I'll go to the café next door which takes cash – the coffee's better too!

But with interest rates coming off rock bottom, buying companies with a decent cash pile can prove a great strategy. If the company you find has a big cash pile *and* profits are rising *and* things look good – well, even better.

How do you find them?

I tend to go through companies that are reporting. I have an idle look through and when I come across big cash, that opens up a share for further investigation.

When I say cash, what I am after is a **net cash** figure.

Pretty much all companies give a net debt or a net cash figure with every full- or half-year report.

I'm no accountant and it doesn't reveal everything, of course, but a decent net cash amount is definitely positive.

Stockopedia and SharePad both list net cash or debt (they use a minus figure to show net cash: without the minus it is net debt). And you can use the traffic lights system on ADVFN to spot it, too (see **The bare necessities** or, for more detail, *The Naked Trader*).

As you already know, I hate big net debt – that's an indication of a share to possibly go short on.

Always check the amount from the latest company statement. And make sure you're definitely looking at the most recent one – if a company has just reported it can take a few days for sites to update. SharePad and ShareScope also feature net cash forecasts.

When I see net cash I smile. It makes me feel it's unlikely anything catastrophic is going to happen. And when there's net cash there's the possibility of a company using that money: for share buybacks, acquisitions or big dividends. All of which should help a share price.

I'm not saying just look at net cash. I'm saying if you find a company with good net cash, it is worthy of further inspection.

Me me me

Here's an example. ME Group, the coin-operated-machine company (formerly Photo-Me), is traded in the **Turn and face the change** strategy. As you can see, its net cash stands at £43.2m – well up on the last time it reported. This is the kind of healthy amount I look for.

	Reported		
	Six months ended 30 April 2022	Six months ended 30 April 2021	Change
Revenue	GBP115.3m	GBP94.6m	21.9%
EBITDA (excluding associates)(1)	GBP40.2m	GBP28.7m	40.1%
Reported profit before tax	GBP19.9m	GBP12.0m	65.8%
Adjusted profit before tax(2)	GBP16.0m	GBP12.9m	24.0%
Profit after tax	GBP16.4m	GBP9.4m	74.5%
Cash generated from operations	GBP29.8m	GBP22.4m	33.0%
Gross Cash	GBP96.8m	GBP95.3m	1.6%
Net cash	GBP43.2m	GBP16.9m	155.6%
Earnings per share (diluted)	4.35p	2.49p	N/A
Interim dividend per Ordinary share	2.6p	nil	N/A
Special dividend per Ordinary share	6.5p	nil	N/A

(1) EBITDA is Reported profit before tax, less total depreciation and amortisation, less other net gain, finance costs and income.

(2) Adjusted profit before tax for the six months to 30 April 2022 is profit before tax adjusted to exclude profit on sale of property and loss on disposal of subsidiary La Wash

(3) Refer to note 8 for the reconciliation of net cash to cash and cash equivalents as per the financial

Net cash for ME Group

If I saw the reverse amount of net debt, I'd be worried. But when you spot net cash, you start your research with a smile.

Another example: when healthcare firm **Totally** reported, its results showed net cash of £15.3m.

Checking with SharePad, I see they're forecasting net cash to rise further over the years under **net borrowings**. (Remember, the minus figure is positive, meaning net cash.)

Given Totally has a market cap of £80m, that cash is quite a decent sum. Similarly, with ME Group's market cap of £380m, £45m is a significant chunk of change.

Beware of property companies and companies relying on net asset values. They often have massive debt but it doesn't matter as they are backed by property or other assets.

Stockopedia has **net fixed assets** close to the net debt column. That can be worth checking but don't assume a company could really sell its fixed assets at this price! I usually cut it by a half at least.

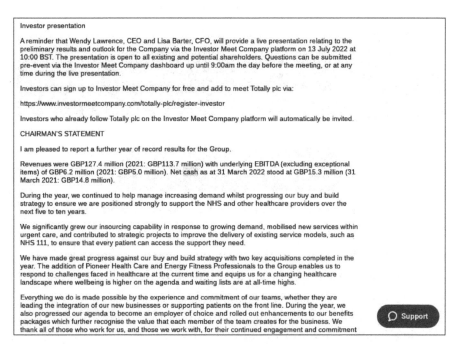

Net cash for Totally

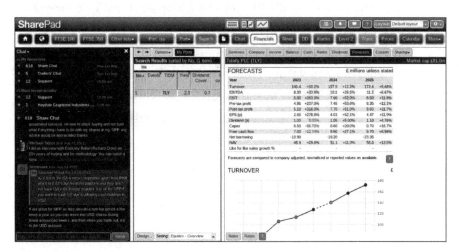

Checking out Totally on SharePad

Anyway, that's why I struggle to value property and companies where the assets are more in things like property than good hard cash. And that's why I tend to leave those types of sector alone.

NT Note! In essence, looking closely at companies with good net cash could make you quids in.

Lessons learned

- Lots of net cash is always a positive. Use it to find companies worth a closer look.

- Cash on the balance sheet means things are going well. It could also mean the company using that dosh to give money back to shareholders (dividends), to buy back its own shares (raising their value), or to acquire other companies (resulting in a bigger and more valuable firm).

- Check the amount of cash in relation to the overall value of the company. If it's 10–20% of the company's value or more, that's decent.

- Be careful with property companies or other firms with assets that are tricky to value. They may have huge debt, but those tricky-to-value assets potentially counterbalance it.

Look at promotion/ relegation shares

Shares are listed on the stock market, but the stock market isn't monolithic. There are lots of different indices of stocks. You could argue they're a bit like the football league. So, in the UK:

- The FTSE 100 is the Premier League.
- The FTSE 250 is the Championship.
- The SmallCap is League 1.
- Fledgling is League 2.

After all, shares get promoted or relegated from these indices depending on how well they are doing. Sometimes, just like football clubs (e.g. my Fulham), they yo-yo between indices.

Why is this important?

Well, a little before it's confirmed who's getting promoted or relegated, shares on the cusp of promotion tend to go up, and those on the verge of relegation tend to fall. (This is mainly true of shares on the 100 and 250.)

An interesting strategy is therefore to buy likely promotions. (You could also consider shorting relegations.)

Finding promotion and relegation candidates

Promotions and relegations happen every quarter: roughly mid September, December, March and June.

How do you find these?

There is a free site, stockchallenge.co.uk. Click 'FTSE Ranking' on the top menu. This brings up a list of all the shares in all the clubs, and you can see which ones are likely to be promoted.

You'll find "Samantha's predictions" there, which highlight the likely moves.

UK StockChallenge

« < > »	2023	Jan 2023	Feb 2023	Hall of Fame	Veterans	Dividend Dates	FTSE Ranking	Contest Schedule	Entry Form	Rules	Contact Us

FTSE All-Share Index Ranking (unofficial guide)
As at close on Wed, 25 January 2023

Rank	EPIC	Name	Index	Price	Mkt cap (m)*	Key
1	AZN	AstraZeneca	FTSE 100	10,810.00	167,504.0	Index entry candidate
2	SHEL	Shell	FTSE 100	2,332.00	163,897.8	Index exit candidate
	BHP	BHP Group Ltd		2,840.50	143,765.4	FTSE 100
3	HSBA	HSBC Holdings	FTSE 100	598.50	119,510.5	FTSE 250
4	ULVR	Unilever	FTSE 100	4,060.50	102,842.7	FTSE Small Cap
5	BP.	BP	FTSE 100	474.70	85,765.1	FTSE Fledgling
6	DGE	Diageo	FTSE 100	3,675.00	83,486.1	FTSE AIM
7	RIO	Rio Tinto	FTSE 100	6,336.00	79,178.1	Unclassified
8	GLEN	Glencore	FTSE 100	558.50	71,736.3	Samantha's Predictions
9	BATS	British American Tobacco	FTSE 100	3,062.00	68,462.2	**ECOR** enters the FTSE Small Cap
10	GSK	GSK	FTSE 100	1,403.60	57,466.2	**HTG** is promoted to the FTSE 250
11	AAL	Anglo American	FTSE 100	3,596.50	48,106.0	**LABS** enters the FTSE Small Cap
	BNC	Banco Santander SA		273.25	45,700.0	**MOON** is demoted from the FTSE 250
12	REL	RELX	FTSE 100	2,353.00	45,059.9	**PHI** is promoted to the FTSE 250
	WDS	Woodside Energy Group Ltd		2,140.00	40,633.3	**888** is demoted from the FTSE 250
13	RKT	Reckitt Benckiser Group	FTSE 100	5,664.00	40,538.8	

Promotion and demotion calls at UK StockChallenge

You could also look near the top of each league. What's getting close to promotion? That share is probably doing well.

The best time to buy is around a month before a likely promotion, as fund managers may only start to buy newly promoted candidates nearer the actual promotion. For example, consider buying early August for the September promotion, early November for December, early Feb for March, and early May for June.

There's usually an announcement early in the promo month, followed by the actual promotion a couple of weeks later.

Consider taking profits a little while after promotion as the effect will begin to wear off.

As ever, you still need to do proper research with this strategy. Despite likely promotion, shares can still be stinkers.

Lessons learned

- Stock market promotions and demotions happen every September, December, March and June. With a bit of digging, you can find the companies likely to be moving – and trade in the right direction before the move.

- Don't hang about after the trade. The effect is usually short-lived.

- Even stinkers get promoted from time to time, so be careful.

Hit the
FTSE 250

I often find investors tend to favour either big companies or very small ones. If you hit trading or investing forums there are tons of threads about massive multinationals – *and* teeny-tiny micro firms.

I get the appeal: there's so much information on the giants out there, and everyone has a view on them. And you can always trade in them. Meanwhile, among the minnows and penny stocks, while trading might be harder (fewer shares are on the market), there are always some hundred-baggers waiting to be found (as well as lots of companies that will go to zero).

The beautiful middle is often neglected – unfairly.

It really is a sweet spot in my opinion. I find looking for shares in the UK's FTSE 250 to be more rewarding than *anywhere* else.

As we've just discussed, the various stock market indices are like football league tables. In the UK there's the FTSE 100, FTSE 250 (the next 250 shares outside the 100), the SmallCap and then the Fledgling. They're based on market values. The higher your market cap, the higher the league you're in.

At current prices that means a valuation of around £4.5bn gets you a slot in the 100, and a cap of around £730m gets you in the 250 club. Under that you're off to SmallCap or Fledgling.

(There is no entry to these leagues for AIM shares – that's because regulation of AIM shares is less onerous. They're in a separate table of their own.)

There are problems with all the indices for me – *other than the 250*.

In the FTSE 100, shares are just too crazy. Traded by day-traders, up and down all day long, as robots kill each other for a 0.25p gain. They've all been analysed to death. There is rarely any kind of edge. The 100 is full of mega companies (often commodity-related). I have little idea of how to value them. These shares generally bear little interest for me.

But with FTSE 250 you get:

- (generally) tight spreads and high liquidity (buy or sell loads easily)
- less coverage and less interest from the big boys (over at the main casino)
- a lot of decent UK companies that no one has really heard of.

This means you can do your research, take a position in a really good one, then wait for the rest of the market to catch up.

Some of my biggest gains have come from FTSE 250 shares, much more than small caps – even though traditionally small caps are considered the place to find big winners (if you pick the right one). I think it's just too risky to buy bigger stakes in small caps due to liquidity issues – it's very hard to buy and sell at decent amounts at the prices offered. But with FTSE 250 shares, you can deal in larger amounts easily.

Loads of quality companies sit there, and if you can get your timing right there are big gains to be made.

You might be surprised by the companies on the 250. Like Rolex seller **Watches of Switzerland**. Or **Telecom Plus**, which owns Utility Discount Warehouse, where I've made many hundreds of thousands thanks to the liquidity on offer.

And it's the FTSE 250 shares that tend to get takeovers more often than any other index. Recently I have had major gains from 250 shares that got a takeover bid. Just a few of these include **Clinigen**, **Ultra Electronics**, **Vectura**, **Entertainment One**, **SafeCharge**, **Codemasters**, **Clipper** and **Sumo**.

My suggestion is, instead of trying to find that tiny company that will find oil in swamp land in Bolivia, try some FTSE 250 companies instead. You could find some hidden gems in there, with much lower risk and far greater pay-off than even the most attractive swamp in the world.

Lessons learned

- The FTSE 250 is a decent hunting ground for potential winners.
- Liquidity is way better than in small caps, so you can go for it with bigger amounts.
- Watch for bids in certain sectors and consider buying companies in said sectors.

Score with your football team

Portfolio construction can be a bit like putting together a football team. You need a defence, a midfield and an attack.

- **Goalkeeper/Defence:** In a portfolio, these are your really solid companies (which should pay decent dividends). They may be boring, but that's OK. No one ever wanted an exciting central defender.

- **Midfield:** Shares that are still solid but speedier, with more room to run fast and attack. Good growth companies, in other words. They are probably slightly smaller than the big defensive shares.

- **Attack:** *Very* fast-moving shares, with lots of room for quick rises. You'll find these from trading ranges, shorts, and catching hold of sudden bursts of growth. These might need to be replaced rapidly by substitutes should they run out of steam.

My team in action

Below are some shares in my portfolio at the time of writing, and how they slot into this way of thinking. Obviously by the time you read this a number will have been subbed!

Goalkeeper

⚽ **Telecom Plus.** A utility and telecoms company. This is a big firm, still growing because rival energy companies have recently gone bust – offering it access to a whole load of new customers.

Defence

⚽ **Sureserve.** Installs energy systems. Its services will always be needed, just like a defender. Lots of dull income and worthy profits – with a great dividend. Wonderfully boring.

⚽ **Computacenter.** An info tech company. A new defender in my team, having just been transferred from a bigger club. Boasts nice slowly rising profits and a handsome dividend. Rock solid at the back.

⚽ **BAE Systems.** A defence company – and a great portfolio defender! Lots of long-term contracts (and being in an area governments are spending more money on) make this an excellent addition to my back line.

⚽ **Bloomsbury.** The *Harry Potter* publisher. This one's a little more attack-minded as a defender. It could go for a run up the wings. Plays quidditch for fun in the off season.

Midfield

⚽ **Indivior.** A US drugs company helping people to quit opioids. Soon to get a US listing, which could spur it on to score a goal or two. A speedy attacking midfielder.

⚽ **Totally.** Frontline healthcare and urgent services. Shouldn't run out of customers. A bigger club might also want to buy it. Makes it an excellent midfielder, with defence and attack in its locker.

⚽ **Redrow.** UK housebuilder. Everyone has to live somewhere, making this defensive in bad times, attacking in good. A skilled defensive midfielder for the mix.

Attack

- ⚽ **Aston Martin (short).** Luxury British carmaker. Despite a Saudi cash injection, its debt problems just keep on mounting, making it a short trade for me – with profits flowing to my portfolio as it declines. An excellent winger.

- ⚽ **ME Group.** Vending machines – from passport photos to laundries. Newly off the subs bench, the valuation of this member of the team is flying as both its main businesses are taking off. A superb striker.

- ⚽ **MS International.** A great attacker, this defence and forgings company won a big contract for its guns. If it can make further progress there could be a lot of goals going in the top corner.

Substitutes

You ought to have substitutes ready to come on when you take a player off. These should be potential trades, companies on your watchlists, shares you are waiting to buy or short, perhaps something you are just waiting for the right time to bring on.

Cards

If a team member gets a yellow card (perhaps getting near a stop-loss), consider taking it off the pitch. Two yellows or a straight red (profits warning), you definitely need to send it for an early bath.

Manager

Er, that's you. If you don't get the team right, you may need to resign and start again with a new team.

The referee

The ref, of course, is the market. And we all know that he doesn't know what he's doing.

My team in summary

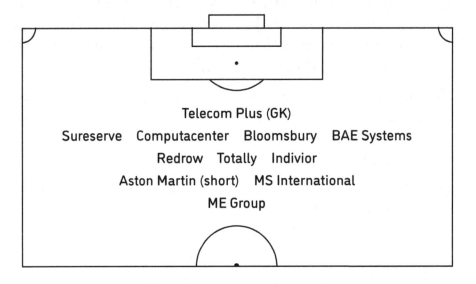

Telecom Plus (GK)

Sureserve   Computacenter   Bloomsbury   BAE Systems

Redrow   Totally   Indivior

Aston Martin (short)   MS International

ME Group

Lessons learned

- Build a balanced team of attacking shares with higher risk alongside defensive shares with nice dividends.

- Always ensure a wide enough selection of players with different qualities!

- You'll want to score a big win – but defence matters, too, and a clean sheet of not too many losers is a must.

Change your mindset

This might sound a rather odd 'strategy' – what the hell do I mean?

After meeting many investors/traders over the years one thing stands out: it is very hard to change anyone's market strategy once they have been using it for a while.

It reminds me of those Gordon Ramsay *Kitchen Nightmare* shows.

You know the format. He visits a crap restaurant. The owner is usually stuck in their ways. Gordon goes in, swears a lot and tries to get them to change. Clean up the kitchen, change the menu, make things simpler, run the place better, make it look nicer... the usual f*cking stuff.

There's always a bust-up mid show when the owner doesn't really want to change things and screws up on the new way forward. But then near the end there's resolution: the owner sees the light.

"I will change my ways," he says, as customers keel over from food poisoning just out of shot.

Gordon gives them some encouraging words once they finally heed his advice. "Everything is so much better now. All you have to do is f*cking stick to it."

But guess what happens most of the time? The owner sooner or later just can't f*cking help themselves and goes back to the old ways. The restaurant goes downhill again.

I suppose it's the old cliché: *a leopard can't change his f*cking spots.*

If you have a spare afternoon while trading (and if you're trading the Naked way, you should!), take a look on the web at most of the restaurants Gordon has tried to change over the years.

It's a disaster.

Most are closed, accompanied to their graves by outraged TripAdvisor reviews. The owners just couldn't help themselves. They knew that Gordon's path was the right one and might have saved their restaurants. But they couldn't follow it for long.

It can be the same with shares and the stock market. I've noticed it now and then. For example, sometimes someone comes to a seminar. They're not a beginner. They've been trading shares for a bit and have already established some kind of strategy. But they're not doing as well as they had hoped. They spend the day with me, tell me they liked it, are going to change their ways and adopt some of my strategies…

Then a couple of years later, I get an email. "I'd like to do another beginner's seminar. Things are worse than ever."

Once someone said that they had got into day-trading, playing forex, bitcoin and a few other of the many dubious things out there that are guaranteed to lose most traders money. This is a million miles away from the common-sense way I teach people to trade. I spend time warning against all of those things!

My advice for struggling traders is similar to Gordon's (swear) words of wisdom for dying restaurants:

- Clean out sinking portfolios (like cleaning a filthy kitchen).
- Simplify everything instead of going crazy with complicated technical analysis (TA) and chart patterns and all that (make the menu shorter).

I don't swear at traders having another tough time, of course, but I do ask what's happened. Usually they say they just couldn't help it.

They knew it was self-destructive but weren't able to change how they behaved.

I think the answer is to change your mindset first.

Mind your mindset

If your mindset is 'I want to make a million on the market in ten minutes', it's pretty hard to change to more realistic trading/ investing, even though that is the only way to eventually make a million (and more) trading shares.

If your mindset is that 'trading is basically a form of gambling', you're going to struggle to stop buying random risky shares, following tipsters and bulletin board and forums. Yes, there's uncertainty to the markets. They're often crazy. But there are reliable, logical methods for extracting profits.

They just require discipline and patience.

There are no shortcuts. Random risks are like having a menu item called 'Meat Surprise' and hoping it generates enough excitement to bring in hundreds of punters to your struggling restaurant.

Here's one chap's account of trying to change:

> "I came to your seminar to learn how to trade sensibly. Up till then I'd been trying to day-trade forex and cryptocurrencies. I found I was losing most weeks but the odd big win kept me going.

> "I stopped after the seminar for a bit and invested more than I traded and made some money but my mind went 'This is not enough, you can make it quicker.' So I reverted back to previous behaviour and day-traded again. I also tried to trade the Dow Jones, which you warned against.

> "I had one or two heavy losses with the Dow and forex. I told myself to stop but it was hard. I want to attend another

seminar with you if I can. I have closed the accounts I was using for my crazy trading and am only going to use my ISA."

This message shows just how hard it is to change behaviour. I am glad to report, though, that this fellow did attend a further seminar – and three months on he hasn't re-opened the accounts he was using to basically gamble. He's trying to make a much more sensible 20% a year. He fixed his mindset.

It shows it can be done, but it's difficult.

If you're losing money trading badly or overtrading or making other mistakes, you have got to get a better mindset. Evaluate your baseline assumptions. What is it driving you to these mistakes? What are you expecting from trading? Fix that and you'll go a long way to fixing your trading.

If you're not ready to fix that, it's seriously worth considering if trading is for you. If you're gambling away family money, you might have a gambling problem. Some people do. It's nothing to be ashamed of. But it is something to stop ASAP. The last thing you want to be is a restaurant that just couldn't f*cking help themselves and goes back to microwaving crap until their average rating declines to 0.5/5 and the receivers are sent in.

Better to close the restaurant right now and try something else if that looks inevitable!

Successful vs unsuccessful mindsets

Here are some examples of trading mindsets that would get Gordon f*cking livid, and good trading mindsets you can replace them with:

Bad

- ☒ I'll never do well at this.
- ☒ I don't deserve success at trading.
- ☒ I have to make money quickly.
- ☒ Failure is the final word.
- ☒ I keep getting things wrong and that dooms me.
- ☒ A few quick risks can change my life.
- ☒ Life is boring, but trading offers excitement.

Good

- ✓ Anyone can make a success of trading if they're disciplined and use common sense.
- ✓ The markets don't owe me anything, but I can apply my methods to put the odds in my favour and over time I will be rewarded.
- ✓ True trading success comes with patience and time, and I have both.
- ✓ Failure is feedback.
- ✓ Mistakes are inevitable – the markets are unpredictable! – but minimising the effects of them is always possible.
- ✓ There's no reward without risk, but risk can – and should – be carefully controlled, as this is the only way to sustainable success.
- ✓ The more boring trading is, the better for my bottom line. I seek my thrills elsewhere.

A coach's view

My wife Elizabeth has been coaching investors and traders for years and has an excellent record at helping those who feel a bit stuck. I figured I should ask her for a few pointers. Of course, to ensure she was in a good mood when I asked, I quickly put the bins out and expertly loaded the dishwasher just beforehand...

So, here's Elizabeth with her top five strategies to give you a successful trading mindset:

1. Be completely honest with yourself. It's part of human nature to ignore what we don't like, to pretend to ourselves that something unpleasant hasn't happened. But if we pretend losses haven't happened, we can't learn from them. Every loss has a lesson in it.

2. Know your strengths and weaknesses. You bring a unique set of characteristics to your trading. If you know what these are, you are less likely to be ruled by them and more likely to be objective.

3. Override your default buttons. If you tend to be impulsive, you will overtrade and make mistakes – and, conversely, if you are a perfectionist and over-analytical, you will hesitate too long and miss opportunities.

4. Beware excitement! Why are you trading? To make money! Don't use trading to fill a gap in your life. If you want excitement, try bungee jumping.

5. Don't take it personally. When you lose on a trade, move on, beware of any old tapes in your mind telling you negative stuff.

I also asked Elizabeth for an example of a trader who got stuck and was about to give up. She had an interesting story to tell (some details have been changed to ensure the person cannot be identified):

" Jared was a proud intellectual man, willing to spend hours on designing and updating beautifully detailed spreadsheets on every company he had ever considered investing in. When we met he was feeling frustrated as all his hard work hadn't led to much success. He was thinking of giving up completely but decided to book sessions with me before throwing in the towel.

Over our sessions Jared told me about all his impressive academic achievements. He had graduated with an excellent degree from Cambridge and spent years working in management at a well-known company before retiring early.

Throughout his life Jared had learned *if I put in the work, I will get the results*. However, none of this seemed to matter with trading. Spreadsheets gave him a sense of control. But he rarely looked back on all the neat columns of figures. He had loads he wanted to do instead of poring over spreadsheets. I asked him: "What is stopping you from doing what you want with your time?"

"I have to work very hard everyday," he said.

"Who says that?" I asked.

"My father," was Jared's reply.

Jared's father had died years earlier but Jared was still running the tapes in his mind of things his father had drummed into him as a child.

Jared had what is called a **limiting belief**. He was so convinced the only way to succeed was constant hard work that he spent his valuable time 'working' at trading but getting nowhere.

Once Jared saw how this belief actually held him back from being a good trader he changed his whole approach.

A few months after our final session, Jared wrote to thank me. He was enjoying life fully for the first time. A bonus was that his portfolio was doing very well as he had applied the Naked Trader principles to his stock picking.

In summary, these are some of the main issues I find investors have:

- fear of missing out

- overtrading

- impulsively trading

- over-analysis – fear of pulling the trigger

- fear of failure

- time management

- fear of success.

If you feel you want to take trading psychology to another level, book a chat with Elizabeth. An initial chat is free – you can book that at her website: coachingwithelizabeth.co.uk

Lessons learned

- If you are stuck in a rut, recognise that you need a change.

- It could be your mindset holding you back. Your beliefs can be misguided and cause stagnation.

- Identify false beliefs holding you back, and replace them with more productive and truthful ones.

- It might be worth finding a trading mindset coach if you can't move forward.

Change your strategy

I f you've been gradually losing money for a while, it's time to change up your strategy.

It might, in theory, be a perfectly good strategy. But sometimes it runs into a rough patch for whatever reason. Or *you* run into a rough patch. Or perhaps it's actually not a great strategy after all – there's a flaw you can't quite detect. (Sometimes the flaw might be gigantic and staring you in the face, as we'll see in a second.)

Whatever the issue, it's important to be open to changing your strategy. You might even want to pause entirely before returning with new strategies.

This is exactly what one investor I came across did. And it worked.

Avi's story

Avi had a decent trading pot he could afford to lose – £150,000 after he sold a business he'd built up.

He decided he wanted to trade it full time. I did suggest it might not have been *quite* enough for that. Don't get me wrong – £150k is a decent chunk of change. But if making 20% a year on your pot is a good effort (and I'd say it is, for an active medium-term trader like me), I wondered if he could manage to live on £30k.

I guess he wondered too. Because he decided to try frequent trading – so frequent it was practically day-trading (where you open and close all your positions within each day's trading session). This is always a bad move.

Avi ignored all my warnings. And began to lose money.

He was sitting at home, with nothing to do after selling his business. Basically he was bored. So he did lots of boredom trades.

'I'm a trader,' he thought. 'Which means I need to trade every day.'

Of course, he simply lost money every day, button press by button press.

When he contacted me, I managed to persuade him to stop. He actually sold everything, went into cash and took a rest. Good for him!

When he went back in, he used more solid strategies. He stopped trying to make quick money. He used longer-term strategies, some of the ones outlined in this book.

If you're reading this and things aren't going well for you, likely you are using strategies that will never make you victorious. You may be trying too hard, putting on too many trades, perhaps some of the *don't* strategies I point out in this book.

> There is nothing wrong with quitting for a bit, cutting all trades, doing something else for a couple of months, then coming back with a clear head and clearer strategies. The markets aren't going anywhere. There will always be opportunities later.

Avi is now making money. Not the big sums he was hoping to make – but he is clawing back some of the lost money, slowly and surely using more sensible strategies.

Losing regularly? You *can* start again. Take a break. Then come back. Use some of my strategies.

Things to cut out

You might not need to stop trading altogether. It could be you just need to cut some stuff out. Here are the biggest typical candidates in my experience. If any of these have made their way into your trading, get rid.

Forex

Please don't go there. I beg you. You will definitely lose.

Trouble is, forex is an easy money-maker for those selling trading systems and 'education'. Forex is big, bright and shiny – international, open 24 hours a day, the largest financial market on earth. You don't even have to research boring old companies. You just have to have a view on a country. It's like the World Cup of money! Or so they'd have you believe.

Forex is all over the internet because people selling such things know that a sucker is born every minute… and a sucker who thinks they can make money trading forex is born every 30 seconds.

The cold fact is, the majority of traders who trade forex lose. The data is unambiguous.

I could have made a fortune luring people into trading forex. I get emails every day offering me big money to "place an article" on my website that will push people to their forex services. They're quite barefaced. They'll even agree when I mention that everyone who tries it loses.

But despite the number of times I bash forex, I can guarantee every month I'll get an email from someone who traded it anyway. It is always a sob story.

Stats show that at least 95% lose on forex trading. My guess is that's really 99%. You're never going to be that 1%!

Day-trading

Day-trading means staying in a trade for less than a day, and going in and out of trades trying to make small amounts here and there. This will never work. Stop it!

As with forex, there are lots of day-trading courses out there run by scam merchants. They typically advertise by showing themselves on a yacht or standing next to a Ferrari or something. That's either money they got from the gullible, or a quick photo snapped just before the true vehicle's owner asks them what the hell they're doing posing next to it like a prat.

Don't be someone who contributes to scam merchants' sports cars. There are many more enjoyable things to spend your money on in life.

A few sensible medium and long-term trades can make you money all day while you simply park yourself in the cinema or on the sofa with a Twix.

Bitcon (spelling intentional)

You may have got lucky if you were one of the first to get in on this Ponzi scheme a few years back – but only as long as you also got out in good time. When you can buy the aforementioned Twix with bitcoin at your local Tesco's, then we'll talk.

Oil and gold

Maybe you'll strike it lucky. But the prices of oil and gold are pretty impossible for traders to predict in my experience. Too many things go into making them. And too many things can impact them at any time.

For traders, they're a casino. If you do strike it lucky, thank your lucky stars, take the profit – and stop.

The casino will happily give you your winnings because it knows you will come back through greed to make more. Then you'll lose.

> A casino likes nothing more than an overconfident trader after a big win. Prove them wrong and quit while you're ahead.

Attending company meetings / meeting the CEO

This makes me unpopular with those that arrange these meetings. Which is a shame.

Some people think it's a good strategy to buy companies after meeting and grilling the bosses. Others merely put a lot of weight on the value of those meetings – but add in other research. The latter is more responsible, but I don't think either approach is wise.

Yes, great, you're getting to look the person who knows most about a company right in the eye and get their perspective on their firm and their industry and what's going on and where things are headed.

It's open! It's candid! It feels like real research – a genuine edge over other investors not doing the hard work of hitting the mean streets of the market and seeing companies face to face.

But what do you think the bosses of these companies are going to tell you? That they have problems? That they're struggling? That some departments are barely holding on? Or that a few key customers are expressing reservations?

You will just get positive spin.

Companies hosting these meetings/events have to pay to talk to you. Successful companies don't really need to spend money talking themselves up to a few private investors.

If you do go, look on it as a social event and don't allow yourself to be influenced by anyone from the featured companies.

Always look at the cold hard figures. Go back to them. Make sure they stack up separately from anything you were told. Never let yourself be fooled by smooth patter.

I learned this the hard way when I started trading. I went to a meet the company meeting, got smooth-talked by someone, bought the shares – and the company went bust six months later! There was nothing smooth about that experience.

Copying trades

Copy-me sites have sprung up in the trading world. These target our laziness. *Hey, just copy a good trader, easy money, no effort!*

The problem is: I meet a ton of traders ever year, and I have *never* met anyone who made money like this.

I have to put it down as 'If it looks too good to be true, it is.'

Or 'If it looks too good to be true, and someone makes a healthy commission in the middle of it all, it *definitely* is.'

The sites get paid on every trade, of course. They definitely make money. As for anyone else… I'm not convinced.

You should also avoid tipsters – people trying to persuade you to pay to follow their tips. If their trades are amazing, why are they making money by selling their ideas?

Not copying trades also extends to *me*. **Don't copy my website trades!** By the time they're live on my site, the trade might even be over.

Instead, copy trading *approaches* – imitate effective strategies, planned properly. That is a tried-and-tested route to sustainable success.

Blokes in pubs

Nothing wrong with blokes in pubs, of course. But if you meet someone down the boozer with a red-hot share tip, you wouldn't go home and stick it in your ISA would you?

Would you?

(Please tell me you wouldn't…)

Same goes for dinner parties. Sorry, if the posh hostess has a nailed-on suggestion for a company to short, the correct response is not to open the spread betting app on your phone but to remind her that you were only asking her to pass the champagne.

By all means, go and investigate such companies further. Same for tipsters. There *may* be something there. But the timing may be all wrong. Or it may just be so they can dump their shares on you. You won't know if you don't do your own research.

Lessons learned

- If your strategies aren't working out, change them up (even if they're good strategies in theory).
- A pause from trading can often help.
- Don't fall for the lure of quick money, you greedy git.
- Avoid all the usual suspects outlined above.
- Think: make big money longer term, rather than losing it short term.

Taming black swans

What's a black swan? After the 2008/9 global financial crisis discussing them was all the rage, because of a finance book by the same name. But – much as it terrifies me – there are traders in the market now who won't have been out of school at the time. So there's no shame in not knowing.

A black swan is (basically) an unexpected event outside normal expectations, and with a big impact.

Ye Olde Financial Crisis of 2008/9 was one. As was **Covid**. We're talking big world-changing events that hardly anyone sees coming. And their effect on markets is significant.

They're one of the harder aspects of being an investor/trader. Everything's been fine for a while – till, bang, out of the blue comes some serious bad news, and the market starts to react unpleasantly.

What the hell do you do? Panic? Sell up? Stick with things for the longer term? Go short?

Panic some more?

How I traded through the Covid collapse

I can tell you what happened to me when Covid hit, and the strategies I used to adapt – and still make money.

The right response depends on many things. One of the big questions is: *How much do you have in the markets, and how much of that can you afford to lose?*

I initially thought Covid was nothing to worry about – something a bit like another flu strain. I was encouraged in that view by the complacency of the markets. I got annoyed when people dropped out of seminars at a hotel in early 2020. 'Wimps!' I thought. 'Covid? Rubbish!'

The day before I was going to host a seminar (which ended up being postponed and taking place online), the Cheltenham races were held in front of a full house. I still thought it was nothing much. I hadn't sold anything. I thought nothing would really happen. And, still, neither did the market! The FTSE 100 was dipping a bit but not greatly. Market reaction had been very small.

Then: hang on.

Boris appears on the TV with a message to the nation, talking about a "lockdown". What! Oh, hang on, this really *does* mean bad things...

First things first

When black swan events like this happen, you must decide on a strategy *quickly* – and be very decisive about your plan.

There is a school of thinking: **'This too shall pass.'** In other words, I am holding my shares for years and years, so I will ignore this and keep holding. This is a valid strategy as long as you are *sure* you're holding great companies.

I don't really agree with it, though.

My strategy is generally: **fire first, ask questions afterwards.**

I pretty quickly topsliced *everything* in my portfolio. By that I mean I took losses/profits on all my shares, cutting them all by 30–50% depending on how risky I thought the share was and how it might be affected by a pandemic.

I also totally sold out of a lot of things I had recently bought.

In any black swan, calmly look at every holding and make some common-sense judgements.

I was thinking: *How will this company be affected by everyone staying at home? Are there any companies that might even benefit?*

After this first step of selling down 30–50% of everything, I ended up with about a million in cash. I think at the time I had about another million left as longs in the market. In hindsight it would have been wise to sell more – though most of the shares I had left were paying 5% dividends.

One share I kept most of was Telecom Plus. People were still going to use gas and electric and their phones, perhaps more than ever – and I would collect the dividends.

Next came the idea of shorting. The idea was to make some money on shares and indices going *down*. I looked around for ideas.

Finally, I rooted around for shares that might gain. I bought a lot of video games companies like Codemasters as I assumed people would sit at home and play games rather than work! A while later I bought some Kingfisher (people will spend the time doing up their homes), which eventually doubled. You will find these strategies in detail elsewhere in this book.

I also bought insolvency companies like Begbies Traynor, at-home drinks companies, gambling and drug companies – anything that could gain with the world confined to home.

It was very important for me to make money from the downside by shorting companies that could be badly affected. So I shorted travel companies like easyJet, Trainline, and Carnival cruises. And restaurants and retailers like the Restaurant Group and Superdry.

Shorting the FTSE

One important idea was to short the FTSE a bit. Here I got very lucky. I didn't even get in anywhere *near* the top! The FTSE was 7700ish and it slipped to 7200 before I started most of my shorting.

When I say I got lucky it's because it literally just went down every day. For weeks. Nearly every day I added to the short as it kept going down. My strategy was to use trailing stops well away from the price.

I took a screenshot or two and you can see my vague strategy for yourself!

Detail	Carnival	(14)	2,263.70	1,444.28	11,471.85
Detail	Pets At Home	(30)	310.05	223.98	2,582.25
Detail	Restaurant Group	(25)	162.81	71.05	2,294.00
Detail	Superdry Plc	(10)	481.38	208.87	2,725.10
Detail	UK100	(240)	6,511.1	5,538.2	233,491.00

A portfolio snapshot, March 2020

The figures in brackets in the second column are the pounds per point of each short. Next column is the price of the short. After that is price at the time the screenshot is taken. The final column is current profit in pounds.

You can see from this screenshot that I was in profit by £233,491 on the FTSE and also had profits on individual shares that I thought would be hit by the virus: Carnival, Superdry, Restaurant Group and Pets At Home.

Here's another shot from a different firm showing profits of £77,000 on another FTSE short.

▶ FTSE 100	7336.8	-265	7044.4	£ +77,490.80	£ +77,490.80

FTSE 100 short profits

This screenshot shows a moment in time quite early on in the shorting. The stake is shown at −265 (meaning £265 per point short).

Here's another, showing my range of shorts – and stops – against the FTSE as they built up:

Market ▲	Reference	Stake	Open	Current	Stop	Limit	P&L Total	Margin
UK100	C28IB391A67U	(30)	6,554.5	6,543.8	6,553.0	-	321.00	981
UK100	C28IB0A1A50U	(25)	6,563.3	6,543.8	6,562.0	-	487.50	817
UK100	C27T6F7DFC3U	(25)	6,790.9	6,543.8	6,795.0	-	6,177.50	817
UK100	C27M65DA1A4U	(20)	6,881.6	6,543.8	6,874.0	-	6,756.00	654
UK100	C27M5B0A172U	(20)	6,888.1	6,543.8	6,873.0	-	6,886.00	654
UK100	C27J2609823U	(10)	6,929.6	6,543.8	6,908.0	-	3,858.00	327
UK100	C25J983E309U	(15)	7,125.3	6,543.8	7,111.0	-	8,722.50	490
UK100	C25J32CE131U	(10)	7,135.8	6,543.8	7,109.0	-	5,920.00	327
UK100	C25J2BBE0D2U	(10)	7,140.8	6,543.8	7,104.0	-	5,970.00	327
UK100	C25J228E067U	(5)	7,144.8	6,543.8	7,068.0	-	3,005.00	163
UK100	C28IBEC1B0BU	(30)	6,553.0	6,543.8	6,552.0	-	276.00	981

My shorts on the FTSE in Covid

Take the (15) stake short – the short was made at 7125.3, the current price was 6543.8, the stop at 7111.0. You can see at this stage I really wanted to ride the downtrend but all stops were around breakeven – a lovely position to be in. I couldn't lose!

Not too soon after this the FTSE really tanked, and I moved all the stops you see in the screenshot down with the market.

Eventually most of the stops got hit around the 5500 mark as the market recovered. Profits were then banked automatically.

Let's say the FTSE went to 6000. I'd still have the 7200 positions open, but the stop would now be in a good profit at 6300 or so.

I wanted to try and hold the positions. At one point I was up £300,000! That's when the FTSE reached rock bottom at around 5000.

I relied on all the stops to get me out unemotionally – and they did. Very roughly I made around £220,000. I don't know for sure as I am not Mr Spreadsheet. But hopefully the screenshots give you some idea.

You can also see from the chart how I *didn't* get in at the top and out at the bottom – a mere part of the move was good enough.

If this sort of black swan event happens again, my rough strategy would be to sell the FTSE or the Dow or whichever I fancy, keeping a trailing stop around 300 (FTSE) points away. That way you don't get stopped out on a spike up, and maintain the short as it goes down.

> An important point to make is that if you start shorting but the event peters out, or the market begins to rocket back up, **get out.** You can really do your brains if you don't.

Shorting in an ISA

One way to make money from market-changing events without spread betting to set shorts is to buy a **short-tracker ETF** in your ISA.

There are a number of ETFs you can use. Generally, I use the **3UKS ETF** these days. You buy it in your ISA just like a share or a fund, and it should rise by 3× the amount the FTSE falls. The reverse is also true. For example, if the FTSE falls 10% you should get 30% out of it.

There is a time element – maybe you won't get exactly as much as three times. But generally it's close to it for me.

You can see from the screenshot here I took from 2020 that I more than doubled my money using the 3UKS – a rather nice 106%. I ended up buying about £131,000, which turned into £270,000. A lovely return from an unlovely time.

ETFs			£270,160.00	17.28%	£131,023.46			
Wisdomtree Multi Asset Issuer Public Limited Company WISDOMTREE FTSE 100 3X DAILY SHORT 3UKS	11,000	2,456.0000p	£270,160.00	17.28%	£131,023.46	+106.1%	Buy	Sell

Shorting in my ISA

Like the spread bet short strategy, of course you *must* get out if it goes against you and the market starts to rise. You buy the ETF just like you would a share. If the ETF trades at, say, 500p and you buy 1,000 just like a share, it will cost you £5,000.

Spreads are tight and there is no stamp duty. The one big difference with spread betting is that the ETF only operates in market hours, not 24/7 (bar weekends) as in spread bets.

There is a sister ETF, the **3UKL**, which does the opposite and goes up three times with the FTSE. That can be used for the Santa rally strategy discussed later in this book.

These ETFs can help to mitigate paper losses from shares still held. Let's say you have a £20k ISA. You've made a profit of £5k but are worried about the markets and want to take out 'insurance'. You could buy, say, £5k of the 3UKS and keep the rest in shares. The market tanks. You double your money on the 3UKS, making £5k. The shares fall in your ISA – but the 3UKS probably covers it. Once the market starts to rise, you can take profits on the 3UKS.

If you haven't used a shorting strategy before it can feel a bit overwhelming at first. I'd suggest going in with *very* small amounts to start off with. And beware of setting stops too close. Indices are volatile and you can easily get stopped out again and again, despite the overall trend heading exactly where you called. In the end my bets were super huge. Can't think I'll ever go that big again until the next black swan flaps its wings.

You may notice that despite the market knowing about Covid, there was *plenty* of time to get shorts in. The market often takes longer to react to events than you might imagine.

I know the above strategy is risky and perhaps hard to take in. But once you've set up your stops to limit the risk of the market turning against you, it can feel remarkably straightforward. Indeed, on FTSE shorts and share shorts, once you are in a decent profit and you have locked in stops at profit, you can actually *relax*!

Lessons learned

- Be prepared to take action on big news and move decisively.
- On a major black swan, shorting may be the only way to make money.
- There's no harm in going into cash for a while – you don't have to trade.

Get out quick

In the last edition of my book *The Naked Trader* I spoke a bit about 'getting out quick'.

The idea is: you bought something. You've done your research, nodded to yourself at how brilliant you were to find this amazing investment, pressed the buy button. Now it's just a matter of time before you make X amount of money and you can brag to your partner/mate/mistress how much you're making from it.

In the unlikely event you're wrong, you set a stop 20% away, which won't be hit anyway because you're so clever. *Wot? I got something wrong? Never!* But what if the share starts to go *down*? Should you stay with it – or should you have another look and see if maybe you were wrong to buy it in the first place?

Getting out quick at such a moment is a strategy that can save you a lot of money.

Here's an example. I bought some **Finsbury Food** in December 2021 at just under 97p. I'd just held an online seminar for my advanced students. We take a vote on every share discussed on the day and this one got the most votes.

Finsbury made cakes and breads and pastries and all kinds of yummy things. That already got me going. Profits were rising nicely, forecasts were good, and there was a decent dividend too. Share price was on the up, and the forward PE ratio looked low. A potential bargain?

Yes, maybe. At the back of my mind there was a tad of doubt. What about rising inflation and logistics problems? However, a couple of people in similar businesses thought price rises could be passed on. So I bought some.

I was looking for it to rise from 97p to 120p. That was the idea. I stuck in a stop of 85p just in case.

And it did start to go up. *Yeah, I know what I'm doing!*

It went up over 100p. That's it, no problem. But then… and only five or six weeks after I bought it… it just kept slowly falling. The order book didn't look good. There seemed to be a lot of sellers about.

I kept reading about inflation being likely to soar, which could hit food prices. Would people really pay a lot more for fancy cakes and baked goods?

The price dipped below where I'd bought it. More grim news on inflation kept coming in. The whole market was beginning to fall after an early January rally.

Instead of waiting I decided to simply **get out quick**.

I sold at just under where I had bought, taking a small loss of under £100.

Hard to do, but essential

It's a surprisingly hard thing to do, getting out quick. It crystallises a mistake. Far easier to keep holding in the hope you didn't, and ignore any negatives.

Why not wait for a stop?

The clue is in the question. If you think something is headed for stop, you know you've got it wrong. At that point, there is no real upside to waiting. In this case it saved substantial losses. The share price continued to fall bit by bit every day and tumbled below 70p by April 2022.

Finsbury Food – an unappetising outcome

> If I'd taken no action my losses would have been painful (though, thanks to the stop, not disastrous). As it was, they were next to nothing.

When should you use a get out quick?

Well, hopefully the above scenario helps. You buy something but the price just keeps falling. You re-look at the buy and realise you missed something. In the above case I took inflation too lightly. And I didn't foresee the horrible war in Ukraine starting at that point – with rising ingredient costs pushing the Finsbury price even lower by April.

Sure, the stop would have got me out – but at bigger losses.

Lessons learned

- If a share price keeps gradually falling daily, the market might be telling you something.

- Re-look at the share. If you now have some doubts, or missed something, or the entire market is steadily falling, or you realise you wouldn't purchase it now, a get out quick can come in handy (even if you have stops set).

Turn and face the change

They say a change is as good as a rest. For a trader, a change is a chance to take *action*.

Often, with a bit of reading and a touch of common sense you can see a company's prospects are changing – which could be time for a trade.

It might be coming out of a recession (or a pandemic). Or perhaps something is causing a sudden demand for its products. Or politics is altering its prospects. Or a lot of things!

But how do you find these?

Plenty of possible ways!

Looking at lists of **breakouts** is one way. For instance, a list of **1-year breakouts up** will show you shares that have moved higher than at any point in the past 52 weeks – a good prompt to investigate further:

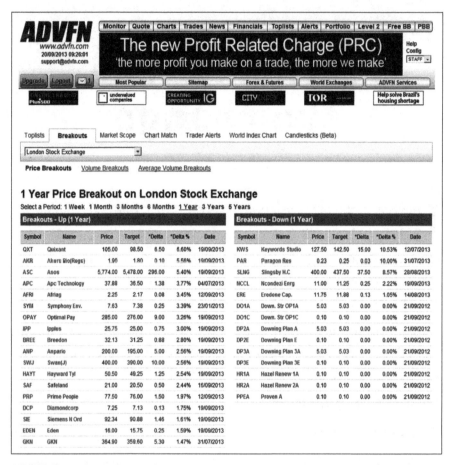

ADVFN breakout examples

Stock screens like the **Top MomentumRank** on Stockopedia are another source of such companies. It looks for the strongest-trending stocks in the market.

Sometimes you might pick up on something in the papers, perhaps an interview with a company boss. Or a profile of an industry in a magazine. It's worth reading morning company reports, too. Something might come up.

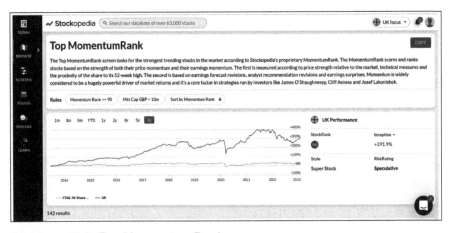

Stockopedia's Top MomentumRank

Photo fantastic

One trade that surfaced for me using this strategy was **Photo-Me**, the photo booth company (since renamed ME Group). I found it via Stockopedia's momentum screen.

I hadn't ever given it much thought before, really. I figured that photo booths were old-fashioned and it was a company that seemed to have little going for it, with boring out-of-date machines. After all, people had phones for photos now.

But I read its trading statement after seeing it on the momentum screen. And I realised: *Hang on, the story has changed here!*

After the Covid lockdowns, people *were* using the booths. A LOT! Everyone was desperate to go on holiday again, and for a lot of people that meant finally renewing their passport (and getting new passport pics) after not bothering with it for a couple of years.

Not only that – the company had a ton of cash (mainly in all those pound coins poured into their machines). And it had launched another business too: coin-operated laundries, including massive machines outside supermarkets where people could wash big items like duvets.

This was a *definite* change in the story. A surge of demand in its old business, and a newish business alongside it bringing additional profits and cash. Plus a rising cash pile and a very good outlook. One of the best possible stories you can find!

But if all that was obvious to see – and the stock was already on the momentum screen – wasn't I too late?

Nope. The good news is, the market often takes *ages* to re-rate story changes – and you can get on even after the story is out.

Here was my plan for this trade:

The plan – Photo-Me (ME Group)

- Buy price: average of 79p
- Target: 100p
- Stop-loss: 66p

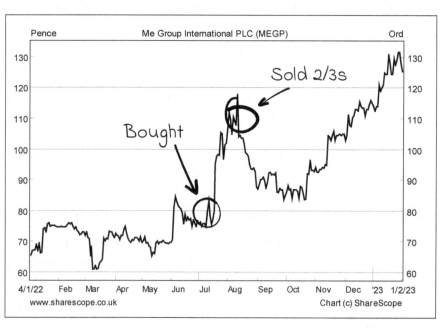

ME Group – a photogenic trade

What happened next

I ended up buying at an average of 79p on 11 July 2022. The rise was so great after interim results on 19 July that I had to part two thirds of them at just under 110p in August 2022; but I still hold the rest as I write.

Shorting bad stories

You can also short shares where a previous good story gradually turns bad. Sometimes a fairy tale turns into a horror story. That's when it might be time to open the spread betting account and put on a short trade.

You'll often find such companies come up on screens designed to pick up on *downward* momentum. But you can also begin to detect such twists and turns from general market news.

One I found that way is drinking tonic company **Fever-Tree**. This was a fantastic success story. Their (very tasty) premium mixers have been hugely popular. Shares fizzed upwards as its little glass bottles stormed into pubs and supermarkets.

All looked good for a long time, until… a plot twist, and the story changed. Just by reading newspaper stories, I realised that the cost of everything they used – from glass to gas – was going up. I read their statements. And they showed a *lot* of negatives.

Massive inflation was biting into margins. The sheer logistics of moving goods took a financial beating. The story was definitely changing. And it produced an opportunity to short.

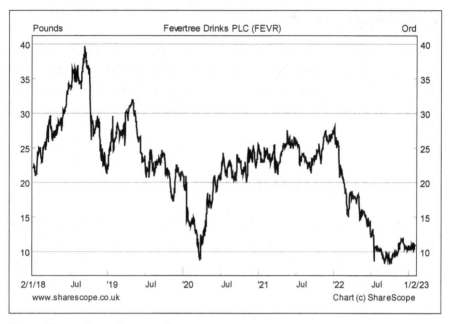

Fever-Tree – from fizzy to flat

Another one!

Another example (and an old favourite) – **Telecom Plus**. This started appearing on lots of upward momentum screens when a story all in the UK are familiar with started breaking – which in turn changed *its* story.

The first story? In 2021–2 lots of small energy firms started going bust because they'd offered customers price fixes that were now lower than the wholesale price of energy. Tons of customers were now looking for new energy deals.

Which changed Telecom Plus's story. Because it supplied such deals. And it had little likelihood of going bust, thanks to a long-term supply agreement with EON. Now it was gaining customers.

The company's statements became bullish – greater ease of gaining new customers meant bigger profits on the way. Higher energy prices and the big re-rating of the government energy cap also played in its favour.

This was an unexpected change in the story of the company. It was easy to snap up shares and keep adding.

The plan – Telecom Plus

- Buy price: 1019p
- Target: 1500p
- Stop-loss: 900p

The shares pretty much doubled from £11 to £22 in just a few months. I'm still holding as I write!

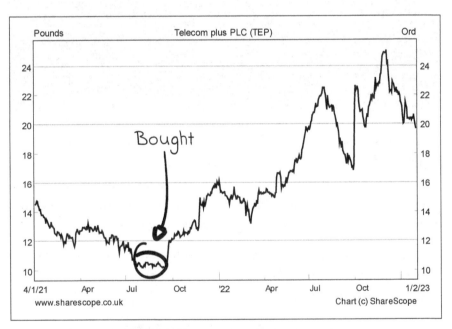

Telecom Plus – electrifying!

Be a detective

You have to be a bit of a sleuth sometimes to pick up on changes in a company's story.

When a company is on its way to becoming a horror story, the first signs are when question marks slowly creep into statements. Companies try very hard *not* to deliver bad news. You'll often only sense it in odd hints here and there. Over time everything just gets slightly worse. Eventually all that 'slightly worse' adds up to 'terrible'.

If you're in a company that starts to show hints of bad things, think about getting out at the first sign of trouble. Remember that they'll likely soft-peddle problems to the extent that they're legally able to.

> Once a story changes, the narrative usually continues that way for a while – whether for good or ill. A share that's rising will usually carrying on rising. A share that's falling will typically keep falling. At least for some time. That's excellent for us traders. You can often keep adding to a position for a while. But don't forget to plan your exit. There's no such thing as a never-ending story in the stock market.

As a market detective, you'll want to read the business pages of the papers. I find *The Times* and *Sunday Times* very good. *The Telegraph* has a very good rolling business news service. Watch for odd stories about companies, things changing. Read the statements when they come out at 7am daily. You might find something.

Use my highlighter idea on previous statements – any red negative words appear? It might be worth checking the company's website too. Anything negative there? Some have a blog, check that too!

Lessons learned

- Always check for clues that something might be changing.
- Have a good look at recent statements for negatives.
- Check 'outlook' statements – anything coming up in the future that looks dodgy?

Be patient
with entry

You know the score: you've found a share you like the look of. You've done all your research. You *still* like the look of it. That makes you smile. But... there is a but.

Two buts.

First, the spread is a little wide. Second, the price is knocking up against a price where it usually fails.

What to do?

Here's an example: mobile-messaging firm **Fonix**.

It's early January 2022. The mid price of Fonix is about 160p. The spread is roughly 5–7 points, though. I like the fundamentals – as said, it's in mobile messaging, which is a pretty good sector. It has a lowish PE and a near 5% dividend and a nice net cash pile.

Most of the boxes I like are ticked. I have also traded it before for a nice profit; I feel like I know it a bit.

BUT!

A look at the chart shows it has got to the 160–170 area once or twice before, *never* got through it – and it then tends to go *down*.

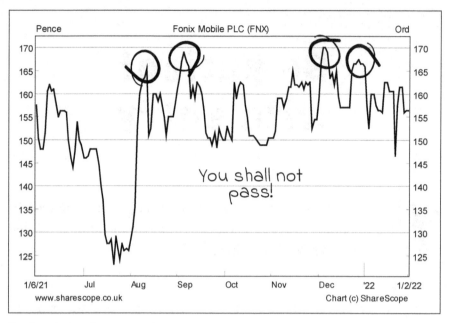

Fonix – bouncing around

Mr Market obviously thinks that's about as far as it should go for now. It's annoying – I want to buy it. But it's got to this price area so many times before and retreated that I know I need to wait.

I *could* buy and plan to get out quick if it drops to, say, 150 – but that is a few percentage points and there's a pesky seven-point spread. Pretty costly.

I note the idea down then set an alert with Stockopedia to let me know once the price gets to about 135. That's because, looking at the price chart in the past, every time it gets to ~135 buyers seem to come in.

I forget all about this idea until one day in early March, I get the notification! Fonix is now available to buy at 130p.

The plan – Fonix

- Buy price: 130p
- Target: 155p
- Stop-loss: 110p

I go in and check that nothing has gone wrong with the fundamentals. Then I buy, making a note to get out quick (if things go wrong) at 122p. The chart shows a decent level of support there. If it dips lower, it probably means something is wrong and I need to quit.

Thankfully, though, it doesn't drop!

It rises fairly quickly back up to the 155p area. Where – knowing the chart – I sell.

Fonix – good things come to those who wait

I did want to hold on in the hope it could break through 160, but the chart couldn't be ignored. I also took a look at Level 2 (not something you necessarily need to worry about as a trader, and a bit complicated to explain in a book, but basically something that gives a snapshot of buyers and sellers in the market at any given time). And Level 2 was weak on Fonix: a lot of sellers were around.

All in all, profits had to be taken.

As it happened, if you look at the chart you'll see that this was the time that it *did* smash on through, before coming back to roughly the same level – and then going on a run beyond, perhaps establishing a new range. An interesting development! There was, of course, no way to know that – and my strategy did what I needed it to. So no regrets here.

Lessons learned

- If you like a share but it looks like it is going down for now – perhaps Level 2 and the wider markets also stink – find the point on the chart where there has been support in the past, set an alert, and be patient.

- Sure, the share may decide to break up, well – so what? We don't want to worry about fear of missing out do we?

Go against the crowd

I t's amazing how often the crowd goes for the same share. You'll often find one company all over discussion forums. But the crowd usually gets it wrong. And that brings a wonderful opportunity – to trade against them with a short. It can really pay off.

I don't really know how a share becomes a crowd favourite or why the crowd picks the worst ones. Usually it starts with an over enthusiastic tipster/guru. Gradually the word spreads. Everyone is in on it. The crowd falls in love, gets confirmation bias and ignores any negatives.

And an opportunity arrives.

If you see red flags emerging despite all this herd positivity, it could be time to step in to short.

> You need to find a company that has a *very* high level of posts and discussions. And you need to then make sure there really *are* red flags there. When you've done that, it's time to trade.

Someone once followed me around a hotel where I was hosting a seminar telling me in passionate detail about their love for a share. I made a mental note: *"Short that one tomorrow."*

I actually once made thousands shorting Rockhopper because someone was so desperate to tell me about it he did so while I was having a wee in the toilets.

My most recent trade against the crowd (at the time of writing) is **Boohoo**, the fashion retailer. The Stockopedia forums were full of posts on it. And that is a decent and sensible forum. But I don't think I had ever seen that many positive posts about one company, led by one or two cheerleaders. Everyone seemed to be in it – but the shares were falling quite quickly. I looked further into it. There were a *lot* of red flags.

Once a successful online retailer, problems were mounting. There were investigations into it paying people below the national minimum wage. There were supply chain problems. High returns. Even a lawsuit from the USA, as well as worries about the impact of throwaway fashion.

Shares fell dramatically over 2021 from 350p to well under 100p. I shorted from around 300p and then more in the mid and lower 250s. When shares crashed below 100p I thought it was sensible to take some profits, which I banked at 98p. I left the rest running, eventually closing out at 32p in September 2022. At such a low price, I figured it might even attract a bid and I was happy with my profits.

The discussion forum herd, of course, held on – and, of course, kept buying more as the shares tumbled. One or two voices of dissent were raised. Those who had done their brains on the shares stayed quiet. You don't want to talk about your disasters, after all.

There are loads of other examples of herd shares gone wrong. Quite a few Covid-related shares ended up being loved to destruction. **Avacta** was one. One bloke even made an "I love Avacta" T-shirt. Another was **Novacyt**.

Boohoo – throwaway fashion

Overall, I actually think it's best to avoid forums if you can. It's tough, as we are a pack animal and we want to follow each other. If you're going to use them, at least make sure you don't follow the herd into share adoration – but keep your eyes open and prepare to short.

Lessons learned

- Find the shares everyone is in and won't shut up about – the more enthusiastic the better – and consider a short. Though do make sure you *can* find problems with said shares, obviously!

- Twitter, bulletin boards, forums are the places to find these.

Avoid
jam tomorrow
shares

Making money on shares over time is also about avoiding bad ones. If you can avoid buying likely duds, you can skip losses (and the impact on your brain) – and that is all to the good. You simply can't win every time in trading. But you can avoid predictable losses surprisingly often.

There are various ways to avoid these stocks.

Jam tomorrow shares are companies with a great story – such as a new technology or a drug or something fascinating that grabs people's attention. But it doesn't make any profit yet, nor is there any sign of profit.

One such story I bought was **Xeros**. This was a total story share! And I really liked the story. It had a method for cleaning clothes using a new technology which required a whole lot less water, reducing the cost of washing. They were getting contracts with hotels too. Ooh! I thought, "Wow! This could turn into a giant."

Unfortunately, the story was more compelling than the finances. There was no sign of profits, and I should have spotted that the company was burning cash and would probably need to carry on fundraising. Luckily for me, stop-losses got me out without too much damage. The shares ended up losing more than 85% of their value.

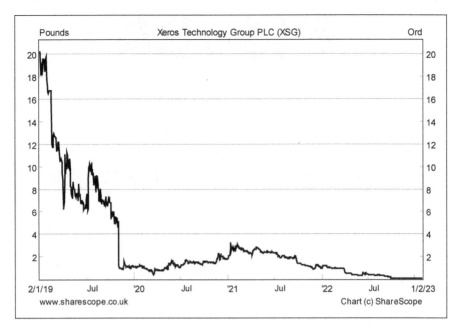

Xeros – a story share with an unhappy twist

Think: if no profits have been made yet, is this just a story and nothing more? Are you being sucked in by a company that will continually need money to keep going?

It's very compelling to buy a story share. They are often companies that have been recently listed. A very recent example at the time of writing is **Pod Point**. I was very tempted by its story. It provides charging points for electric vehicles. Well, surely this a big growth tale! My finger was itching to buy.

But then I looked at stories around the IPO. There was no sign of when profits might come in. It was all waffly. Trading statements said things like "We want everyone to have a Pod Point charger." Good for you! But there were no figures. And what about competition? How about margins?

I learned from past tall-tale trades and didn't buy. I decided to be patient and wait. I could always buy in the future should profits be mentioned! We'll see.

Lessons learned

- Beware of a great story not backed up by profits.
- Watch out for loss-making companies.
- Don't buy if there is no sign of future profits.
- Can this company run out of cash?

Look for longer-term income

O
f course we'd all like to have portfolios where every share doubles in a year – or preferably a few days. Hell, a few hours! But folks, this ain't going to happen. It just doesn't.

But guess what does happen all the time – indeed every year, like clockwork? Companies pay some of their profits back to shareholders in the form of dividends. A number of companies have a track record of doing this for decades. Some even manage to slightly raise the dividend every year too. Like a snowball rolling down a hill, all that money adds up.

I've held some of these companies for years. And every year they've shaken a little more money into my portfolio for very little risk.

This is a good little strategy to use alongside others. It won't shoot the lights out, but it adds some security. Across all my trading accounts, my dividends tot up to about £120,000 a year.

If you have a bad year with shares, you'll find a 5% dividend will make up for a lot of any capital loss.

I'm talking reasonably defensive shares that pay out 5% or so. Shares that aren't going to go bust. They may go up and down over time, but nothing radical (and you can use those moments to pick up a few more).

Let's take good old **Telecom Plus** again. Ultra defensive as it makes profits from people taking its broadband, phone, energy, insurance and suchlike. And it has a long-term energy supply agreement – if the oil price goes crazy, it isn't affected. Everyone has to use the services it offers. This makes it nicely defensive. Over time I even made capital gains on the shares too.

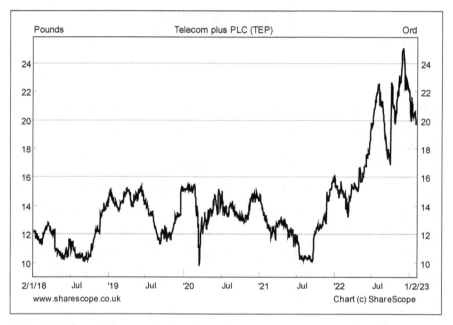

Telecom Plus – slow and steady

But let's take the chart from the last five years as an example. You can see quite simply it goes between 1000p and 1500p with the odd foray to 1600p when it gets excited.

I try and buy it near the bottom of the range and sometimes topslice a bit near the top.

In the meantime I pick up around £20,000 a year on my holding.

Let's take another example: housebuilder **Redrow**.

While housebuilding shares vary with market sentiment, housebuilders *do* supply something everyone has to have (unless you like caravan living). Take the five-year chart and (ignoring the 2020 Covid year) Redrow shares roughly cycle from £5–£7:

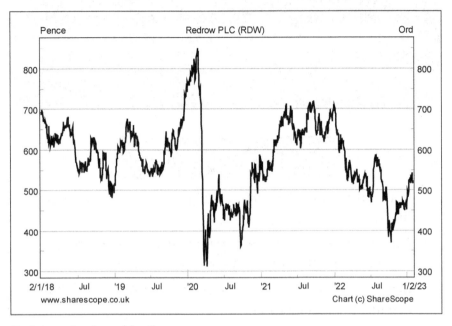

Redrow – back and forth

Like Telecom Plus you could keep picking up the shares near the bottom of the cycle but even if you don't you're getting nearly 6% income here with low risk.

Now imagine half your ISA portfolio is defensive, with shares like these held longer term for the income. You can then play more aggressively and look for capital gains with the other half of your portfolio.

There are lots of articles around on compounding interest and how that works. Have a google of those to see how powerful dividend income can be.

Having held Telecom Plus shares since 2001, my rough estimate is I've gained about £400,000 in dividend income over a couple of decades. Not bad – and there's been capital growth too.

Beware of any share offering much more than a 8% dividend. When something seems too good to be true it always is, and it could be the share had a warning which screwed up the share price, giving an unrealistic ongoing dividend. Treat anything over 8% with suspicion!

Lessons learned

- Have a look around at shares paying 5%. Then take a look at the five-year chart.

- Can you find some nice defensives that pay out? Then try and buy them near the bottom of their trading range.

- Obviously not every single one will work out, but you should find that the majority will.

- And remember, if this is in your ISA, all this income will be tax-free for you.

Conquer confirmation bias

Sometimes a trading statement can change everything regarding a share's likely future.

If you've been long or short of a share for a while you might have **confirmation bias**. In other words, you've become so fixated on the idea that the share is great (if you are long) or crap (if you're short) that you just can't change your mind even if the facts change.

You need to be prepared to change your mind – and quickly. It will save you from losing your profits on a trade – and maybe even provide you with another trade in the opposite direction.

A good example of this for me was **Superdry**, the mid-market casual-wear store. I was short of this one for years! From 425p all the way down to 110. My reasons were poor sales and a debt that was slowly piling up, then inflation worries. I suspected it might even go bust, so shorted some more!

But a statement on 22 December 2022 changed everything. The company announced it had secured a new funding facility – a huge one of £80m. The story I had traded on – that they were going bust – was now definitely not going to happen, at least not for ages. Furthermore, its net debt had come way down – nearly halved, in fact – and store revenue had increased.

I scrambled to close all my shorts, banking a considerable profit.

But I didn't leave it at that – I went long! I made a total switch because of the new information.

Before this statement my mind was full of 'It's going bust, its debt is increasing and no one wants to buy its clothes.' I could easily have stuck to my guns and stayed short. But no – this was important new info that changed things. So much so that the shares looked like a buy to me.

I had closed all my shorts and bought the shares within 15 minutes.

This paid off – after banking very nice short profits, the shares began to move a lot higher.

Superdry – surprise!

It's not just good news that can change things, of course. If a share you're long on gives out a horrible profit warning and the share falls well below your stop-loss overnight don't use that as an excuse to stay with it! It's usually best to change your long confirmation bias on that too.

An example of this for me was recruitment firm **Gattaca**. I bought it at 120p in December 2021 with a stop-loss of 105. Sadly for me a profit warning the next month in January 2022 sent the shares way lower – and below my stop.

Without hesitation I closed the trade at 95p, taking a loss of £1,245. Just as well I did – the shares ended up going even lower.

Gattaca – gettaca the hell outta there

The temptation was of course to stick with the shares. *"They'll come back up!"*

The story changes on a holding? Take action!

Lessons learned

- Always be prepared to change your mind – and fast – on new information.

- Don't let confirmation bias keep you in a share going the wrong way.

- Don't hesitate to switch from long to short or vice versa on new news.

- Get out on a warning even if it opens well below your stop-loss.

Look for multiple income streams

On going through company statements, I do like it when I find a firm with its fingers in a few different pies. The ideal is a company with revenue coming in from multiple areas, with potential for one of these to grow.

I like this because if one of the company's sectors runs into problems, other sectors going well should help shield the company.

A company in just one business is fine – but what if that one business faces a giant problem?

Take Boohoo: online clothing and nothing else. If anything goes wrong with that, the whole company gets battered.

A more robust company would be something like **MS International**. I noticed in a statement on 7 December 2022 that it had various divisions: petrol station superstructures, forging, defence and corporate branding.

And, I noted, all of its sectors were going well and making profits. Pleasingly, net cash had risen strongly from £15 to £23m. It had a lowish PE ratio too.

But what caught my eye was the massive potential in its defence division (yet to make a profit). The company said it was trying to win a contract from the US for its naval gun system. The company called it a potential "great prize" and said it was developing various gun systems.

Buying a company like this is kind of like getting a free shot.

If MS International didn't sell its gun system, well, never mind – the other divisions bring in money. If it *can* sell the systems, then you've hit a jackpot.

In other words, this is a kind of trade where you should get most of your money back if it fails.

I bought 1,000 shares after this statement at 387.5p on 8 December 2020.

The jackpot got hit quicker than I imagined. On 23 December it won a £22m contract to supply its defence system – and said others could be in the pipeline. Shares soared 40% on the announcement. I topped up and now expect to hold for at least the medium term. After all, if it sold one lot, the chances of it winning more contracts are pretty good!

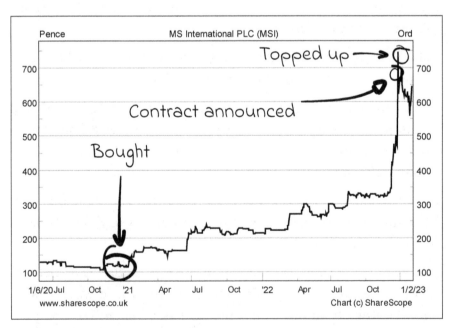

MS International – going great guns

One thing to always check with companies that do more than one thing is whether they have enough cash to fund keeping those fingers in all those pies. If they have a lot of debt, it could cost them to service a new business – meaning they might have to raise a lot of new money at a discount.

Lessons learned

- It's always worth looking closely at companies with different income streams.
- Check they have net cash rather than large debt, though.
- The dream is a company with a number of solid sectors and the chance of outperformance in one or two (supported by a good balance sheet) – you're basically getting a free bet on the upside.

Take an interest in IPOs

New issues or initial public offerings (IPOs) can be tricky things. I've met traders who are up and running and pretty au fait with their trading but come a cropper with these.

I do think it's a difficult area of the market, but having bought and sold these for many years I think I have finally come to some sort of conclusion!

First of all, it's just a fact of life that new issues are hit and miss. Sometimes they are absolutely terrible and sometimes they are good value. Recently there have been a lot more stinkers than good 'uns.

But how do you know which is a stinker?

It's difficult. Annoyingly, new floats sometimes come on and it's hard to even find out what their profits/losses are.

Some come onto the AIM market, some on the main. Some are tiny, some are big.

I've discovered a few ways to try and work something out... but recently I've had more joy shorting new issues than buying into them!

Indeed, some quite spectacular successes. Over the last three years (at the time of writing) I've made over £100,000 shorting the worst ones.

The good news is there is generally no rush to go short – new issues actually tend to go up for a while before the markets realise they are right stinkers!

What red flags are there to short a new(ish) issue?

Look for sketchy details on profits. Some newer small ones don't even give you any figures. But even if they don't you *can* find them. I usually end up at the Companies House website where you can buy the details for around £2.

Check:

- Is there big debt?

- Is 'EBITA' the first figure you see at the top? EBITA (earnings before interest, tax and appreciation) is usually fudged. It's designed to make you believe profits are bigger than they really are.

- How much are directors selling into the new issue? Are directors also selling not too long after it's floated? Perhaps the market the company is in has peaked and the directors are trying to cut and run. Are you buying when insiders want out?

- And, importantly, what's the market cap of the new float and does the valuation look way too big compared to pre-tax profits?

Time for an example or two.

One of my most recent shorts in a new issue was fintech company **Wise Group**.

I had a quick read through the admission document. The company was listing with a market value of more than £8bn, which would see it get in the FTSE 100. It didn't take me more than a minute to think: "This is a short."

An £8bn valuation with pre-tax profits at just a paltry £40m!

On the plus side, there seemed to be a lot of cash, at £3.3bn. And profits and cash were both rising.

But... but... £8bn value. *How?* I took the £3.3bn cash out of the market cap – call it £5bn then. A £5bn value on profits of £40m? That's more than 100×.

OK, profits *had* doubled recently. Let's say profits double again and come in at £80m next time. That's still a crazy valuation of over 60×.

I couldn't see any reason for the bonkers valuation and happily shorted soon after the listing at 1016p in October 2021.

This proved a wise move! It wasn't long before the shares halved, going under 500p – giving me a fabulous profit on the short. And frankly even with a halved market cap it *still* didn't look cheap!

Wise Group – profiting from an unwise valuation

Another one!

Another example? Online greeting-card company **Moonpig**.

This one was floated at a valuation of £1.2bn in 2021. Shares promptly raced a lot higher and soon the valuation was £1.5bn.

I sat there in disbelief when, soon after the float, the company reported profits of just £32m and a massive net debt of £115m!

How on earth could this company be worth £1.5bn?! To my mind it would be lucky to be valued at 15× its profits. Call it £500m.

I shorted.

Shortly after this, there was a massive sell-off of nearly 20m shares by big company shareholders. The pandemic was also starting to wind down. Moonpig's main business was selling greetings cards you order and customise online, then get delivered to the recipient's door. As things went back to normal, people would probably be happy to return to buying cards in shops.

These were two additional reasons to short. I was therefore very happy with my trade. And sure enough, this short worked well and the shares eventually halved.

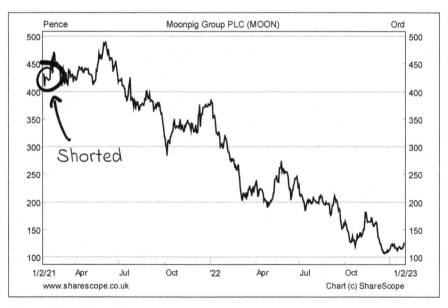

Moonpig – oink oink

I mention a few more IPO stinkers I shorted elsewhere in other strategies in this book. Good examples include Trainline (directors selling like crazy), the AA (massive debt) and Aston Martin (massive debt again).

Now onto IPO buys.

IPOs to buy

When it comes to IPOs I want to buy, I'm looking for companies that seem genuinely good value. For example:

- The market cap doesn't look crazy compared to profits.

- Debt is low.

- Maybe there is even cash.

- The business is growing and has further room to grow.

- It doesn't look like directors are just trying to cash in.

I came across a good example of this in late 2021 with the 'brilliantly' named **Facilities by ADF** (why not just ADF?!). This company provides outdoor facilities for TV/film production companies. It actually seemed to be floated at a reasonable price.

The company was floated in January 2022 with a price tag of £38m. Pre-tax profits for 2021 were £4.2m. That appeared decent value to me: under ten times profits to market cap. Its forecast for 2022 was £5m profits. The company also suggested it was boom time for its facilities. And it had more than 30% of its whole market.

At last: a valuation that seemed reasonable compared to some floats!

There was no sign of massive director selling. TV and film production were all back after the peak of the pandemic, and lots of rival streamers all needed content.

I bought and kept adding as the shares rose. Then in early 2022 the company produced a lovely 'ahead of' statement. (See **Trade the phrase 'ahead of expectations'** strategy.) Perfect!

I had managed a nice profit. But then the entire market fell, and with it went my shares. My stop was hit for a loss. Far from perfect!

In a bad market I managed to pick some shares up again. I hope to keep it as a longer-term buy. (A stop-loss is still in place just in case TV productions fall out of fashion.)

Facilities by ADF – a felicitous trade

One more point to make about IPOs. When shorting you may find it hard to get a short on in the very early days of a float as the spread betting firms struggle to what they call 'borrow stock'.

But there's no need to rush a short anyway.

Let's sum up for those of you with a lack of concentration who skip loads of bits:

Lessons learned

- Only buy into an IPO if you are certain it's still a growth market and directors aren't trying to cash out at the top of the market. Make sure the valuation looks sensible.

- Remember the red flags: too high valuation multiple, use of EBITA, director sales, high debt.

- Lots of red flags and an unreasonable valuation = go short!

Trade the range

An interesting strategy is finding a share which has been trading in a range. It's a nice one, as it gives you the option of a bit of quicker money but also the chance for a longer-term hold should it break out.

My best recent example as I write this is **Airtel Africa**, a telecoms and mobile money firm serving 14 African countries. As you can see from the chart here, from January 2022 it traded in a bit of a range – kind of low 130s to the 160s.

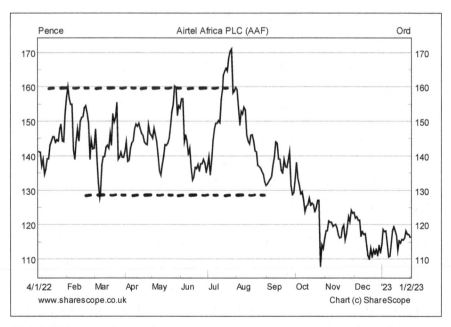

Airtel Africa – at home in a range

Hopefully you can see this quite easily, we even put some lines in for those of you a bit knackered today.

What does this tell us?

The 'market' thinks the shares are worth more than the early 130s when they bounce down there – but once they get to 160s? Meh! Maybe too much for now.

All looks straightforward, but there are some things to check off before entering this kind of trade.

First off: the spread! There is *no* point trying to do this with a tiny small cap. Spreads suddenly widen and they are too illiquid to get enough to bother with.

You've got to clear two lots of spreads on the buy and the sell, limiting any profit. On top of that, with low liquidity you may struggle to buy and sell enough to make worthwhile money, given small caps are riskier.

Try and find a share with good liquidity and tighter spreads. Realistically, you're looking at something on the FTSE 250 upwards – market caps of £500m plus.

Airtel Africa fit this criteria perfectly. Market cap of more than £5bn, tight spread, easier to make a decent sum, less risk of a share collapse than a small cap.

Obviously you want a decent share with long-term prospects anyway. Fundamentally, Airtel Africa's profits were rising, and there was a dividend of nearly 4% (which shows confidence).

What were the risks here?

There was quite a big debt, but within the parameters outlined in *The Naked Trader*. And it had substantial net assets; a bust looked unlikely.

As a trading-the-range story it was a good one. You could buy in the 130s, sell in the 160s. Short in the 160s, buy back in the 130s, etc.

The best place to put a stop-loss is just under where a firm tends to get bought up. In Airtel's case, the lowest price tended to be 132p, so I chose 128p, giving it a little room (always useful, especially if spread betting, as firms add a little extra to the spread).

When trading the range, you have to be careful regarding results and trading statements. What if you are short and a company issues a great report or vice versa? Well, arguably a guaranteed stop on a spread bet could help. (And in general I play trading ranges in a spread betting account.)

I never went short of Airtel Africa, but gained some valuable income trading it on the upside from the lows.

I bought these for 133p on 23rd June 2022. The idea was to play the trading range and hopefully exit in the 160s. Stop at 128p.

The plan – Airtel Africa

- Buy price: 133p
- Target: 160s
- Stop-loss: 128p

What happened next

This trade worked perfectly – a nice profit taken.

After this trade in Airtel the shares fell *below* the trading range. At that point, it was time to stop until another range established itself.

Airtel Africa – I bless the trades down in Africa

Another one!

Another trading range example which worked well was **Spire Healthcare** (also traded in the **Talk to the staff** strategy).

Again, if you look at the chart you can see a rough range – in this case from June 2021 onward of 210 to close to 250. You could have bought a few times in the early 200s and taken profits near 250.

It ticked all the boxes for a trading-the-range strategy: very liquid, not too big a spread. Easy to put a stop in at 197p every time you go long in the early 200s.

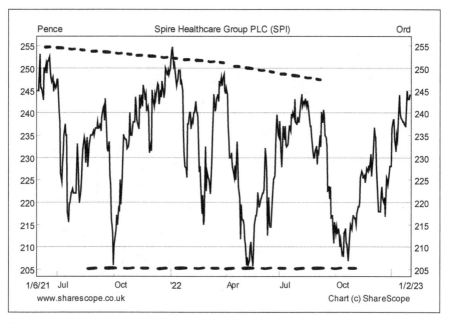

Spire Healthcare – a rough range

What to look for

What you're really looking for is a share that begins to look very cheap at the bottom of the range. If you are looking at a share with a bigger spread – but it's over a market cap of £500m – you may find the larger spread is because it's market-maker-only for some reason, so check the trades. The real spread could be small.

An example: **Team 17**. This video games firm looks like it has a 15-point spread but in reality buys and sells were at just a 2-point spread. It began to establish a rough 385–450 range. I bought some at 385 in May 2022 and sold at 460 just a month later for a gain of nearly £800.

Then I tried to repeat the same trick just a month later, as the trading range pushed it down once more to the exact same 385 level.

I bought at 388p this time on 24 June, awaiting another rise to the 450s.

Team 17 – history repeating

Lessons learned

- Watch for companies trading in a range and see if you can trade them up and/or down over a shorter time frame.

- If a trading range breaks up or down, re-consider. If it breaks *up*, there is potential to stick with the trade for longer-term gains. If it breaks *down*, beware and leave alone, unless you happen to be short of it.

- Always stick a stop in a little below where support is.

- It's always worth looking to see if one of your favourite shares has developed a trading range. They're excellent trades to have in your locker as a full-time investor.

- When you're screening for new shares, have a good check of the chart. Is there a trading range there?

Be a
Dragon

It doesn't matter how long you've been doing this, sometimes your finger will hover over the buy button but something is bothering you.

Is the share you're about to buy *really* realistically valued, or are you buying something that's too expensive? Or has too many problems?

If in doubt with any share, submit it to the *Dragons' Den* test. (If you're reading this in the US, think *Shark Tank*.)

What you have to do is pretend this share is a company standing in front of you asking you for your money.

I quite enjoy imagining being Peter Jones, one of the UK tycoons grilling would-be entrepreneurs in the *Den*. For a brief moment I can pretend I'm a tall, handsome, well-dressed guy. Then it's back down to earth. (Us short bald blokes really do have it hard. Best I could do was either be a share dealer or a violent bad guy on TV.)

OK, you're Peter Jones. In front of you is some sweaty guy with a nervous business partner – neither have a clue what their figures are or what they might make as profit over the coming years. If you're Peter you tell them how dare they come in with a 'crazy' valuation. They are sent on their way.

What Peter is after is a set of profit figures, a company valuation, forecasts for the next couple of years. Then he has to figure out: *Will he get a return if he puts some money in?*

It's exactly the same position you're in as an investor. It's simple, really. Is the business actually worth its valuation?

Let's say Aston Martin came in with a pitch.

Approaching the Dragon

"Hey Peter. We make amazing cars for people with small dicks."

Peter thinks: sounds promising. "Tell me about your profits and forecasts," he says.

"OK, Peter," says Aston Martin. "Well, er, we are probably going to make a loss of £387m this year, but in 2024 we're only going to make a loss of £22m. Oh and our net debt is over a £1bn. We value our business at just £700m."

Peter would go ballistic. "You come in here wanting £700m when you make a massive loss and a big debt. I'm out!"

Before adding: "Oh, and I have a big one by the way."

You see, this valuation just looks too high. Plus their forecasts are for lower losses, but can we believe those? Under the *DD* test, Aston is obviously uninvestible. I shorted Aston Martin myself, and made nearly £50,000 from it.

Next in the *Den*?

"Hi Peter, I'm from ME Group, we operate photo booths and laundry machines."

"Hmm," says Peter, "aren't photo booths past it?"

"Not at all," says ME Group. "Since holidays opened up again, business is rolling in. Everyone needs passport pix and people find using the booths easier than trying to get the right pic at home. And people love our laundry machines. Pop your duvet in outside the supermarket, do your shopping, come out, nice clean duvet!"

"OK," says Peter. "How are your figures looking?"

"We made a profit of £48m this year and in 2024 we reckon we will do £54m, growing nicely. We have net cash of £45m. We think we're worth £400m."

"So," says Peter, "you're asking me to pay 8× profits. And you have £45m cash. I'm in!"

Aston Martin and ME Group – two very different companies. One I am sure Peter would invest in, one he wouldn't. It is simply about the future, and does the market cap of a company look sensible or outrageous in light of it?

Two more entrants

OK, two last entrants into the *Den*…

"We're a pretty boring company actually," says the pitcher. "We do things like install gas appliances and put in new meters, all those unsexy but essential things. We have loads of contracts."

"Figures?" says Peter.

"We've increased profits every year since 2018," says the pitcher. "We're making £16m now, we expect £20m by 2024. Oh and we have cash too, might be up to £30m by 2024."

"And how much are you asking?" says Peter.

"We want an investment that values us at £142m."

What would you say as a Dragon?

Here's what I think Peter Jones would say:

"Your area of business may be tedious but your figures are anything but. Profits are always going up, there's cash, I'm only paying 7× your 2022 figure. Yes, I'm in!"

This share is **Sureserve** – and I was in too! It was a sensible valuation for a quietly growing quality business.

And, finally, now it's a *Dragons' Den* repeat from 2016.

The presenter pitches: "We have a great business, we rescue people whose cars have broken down, and also sell insurance."

"That's a steady business," observes Peter.

"Yes, we're going to make £150m next year."

"Sounds good," says Peter. "Any debt?"

The presenter looks a little sweaty and nervous.

"Well, erm…"

"Spit it out!"

"About… £2.8bn."

"Did you say *£2.8bn?!*" shouts Peter. "You come in here wanting money for a company that owes BILLIONS. I'm out – and you can get out!"

Well folks, that company was **the AA**!

It floated at around 400p a share in 2016. I shorted it like crazy all the way down, making over £40,000. As Peter would have pointed out, with that debt it wasn't worth much.

It eventually got taken over at… 35p!

I hope I've hammered home the point here. *(Yes Robbie, got it, finish up now.)*

Lessons learned

- Pretend you're a tough-nosed investor like one of the big names on *Dragons' Den* or *Shark Tank* before pressing the buy button on a trade.
- Does the valuation look reasonable given likely profits (or losses) and debt?
- If that company was pitching to you personally, would you buy in?
- If so, buy the shares. If not – you're out!

Buy quality (and a bit of momentum)

This really should be top of your strategy list – buy a quality company.

It amazes me the number of people who are more interested in the highest-risk tiny shares hoping to get a 'multibagger' (a share that multiplies in value many times over).

It hardly ever happens and they usually end up doing their brains.

They buy little oil exploration shares, obvious frauds, gold miners. Usually companies making losses with no signs of ever making money.

If you buy quality, at the very worst, you shouldn't lose a massive sum.

But what is 'quality'?

There are a few things that tick the quality boxes for me:

- Barring the Covid years, longer-term rising profits is a tick. As is a decent rising dividend (shows quality and confidence).

- Add in a nice rising cash pile with no major debt on the horizon.

- Perhaps a well-known company that people trust. Directors have been there for years building the business.

- It isn't new, and doesn't have a 'jam tomorrow' story, and isn't failing to make profits. It also doesn't have debt.

- It should be a big and strong player in its market.

Where to look for quality?

Stockopedia has some decent screens, such as its **Top QualityRank** – a score out of 100 based on quality criteria of investing luminaries like Warren Buffett, Joseph Piotroski, Edward Altman and Messod Daniel Beneish.

This includes looking at risk of bankruptcy, earnings growth and the strength of the business franchise.

It's worth taking a look at those with the best scores.

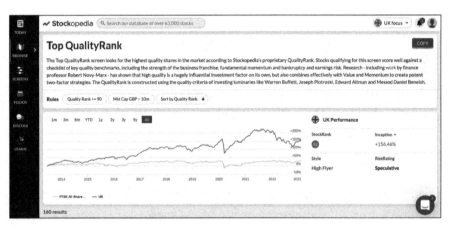

Stockopedia's Top QualityRank

Just because a share gets a good score doesn't mean you just buy it up! You have to do your research as always. After all, the rating comes from a computer algorithm. Be sure to do the usual checks, even on shares with quality scores.

Also check: does the score take into account current market conditions? Let's say a pub group gets a good score. Great, but what if inflation is high, wages are going up and no one wants a job in the industry because all they want to do is be on *Love Island*?

I find it's worth adding in a bit of momentum to this strategy. If you have quality and a share is rising, that adds a bit more confidence. Well, there must be some solid buying for the share to be rising.

For this, it's worth looking at Stockopedia's **Top QM Rank** screen.

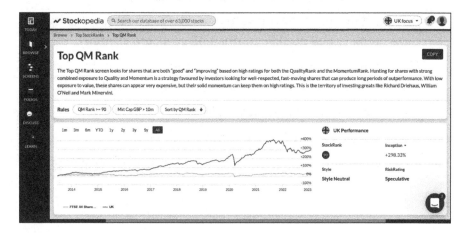

Stockopedia's Top QM Rank

The idea is to combine quality with momentum. Getting a quality share with momentum could well pay off.

But you have to be careful – has momentum taken a good quality share too high?

A warning sign that even a quality share has gone too high could be a too high PE, or high PEG (see **Buy lower PEs and low PEGs** strategy). Or maybe it's up 25% or more but there's a statement due: you could be buying just as people decide to take profits.

There can be a lot of weighing up to do.

I'll look at more screening strategies in this book, but these two screens are a decent place to start.

If you scroll down the shares brought up by the screens you can click on any of them for a summary of what they're about. That means you can quickly dismiss any sectors you don't like without digging any further.

Lessons learned

- Traders don't need to reinvent the wheel or seek ridiculous risks. Seek to buy quality companies as a core strategy.

- That means long-term rising profits, no debt, solid management and products – and other quality metrics.

- It also helps if others are buying into the share already.

- Check the PE and PEG haven't gone too high.

Don't put too much money in

You very much need an overall strategy for handling how much money you're putting into the markets.

My main view is: do not overdo it, ever. Even when things are going well.

Actually, *especially* when things are going well.

How much should I have in the market?

I get asked this a lot. I want to say: Look, I'm not Martin Lewis the money managing expert.

We're *all* very different. Some of you will have commitments (partners, families, etc.) which makes it harder. Some of you won't have commitments and can take bigger risks. And some of you just have fear of commitment...

The main thing is – and I know it is a cliché – but ask yourself really, truthfully, can you afford to lose 70% of the money you have in the markets?

Seriously!

What if 70% of it disappeared overnight? Could you still pay your mortgage? Could you meet all your bills? Would your standard of living go down?

If it would – you've got too much in.

Cut!

Look at what you have in the market right now. Work out how much you will have left if 70% of it disappears. Now. Be honest. Would that be the end of your world? Would you have to cut back or struggle?

Bring your exposure down to levels where if you lost the money you're still smiling and all will be fine.

The thing is, *I know people who have lost 70% or more.* One guy I met had £1m and lost 80% of it. It ruined his life. Some people I've met kept their losses from their partners. Marriages broke down.

In a down market – especially if you're in smaller companies – you can *easily* lose as much as 70%.

One chap at a seminar admitted he'd bought £250,000 of Boohoo shares at 350p. And he carried on holding them, stubbornly refusing to sell as they fell. He said he was buoyed to keep holding because internet tipsters said to do so.

There was no point in berating him about why he hadn't sold or used stops. It happened. He lost most of his money as the shares dived to under 80p. And it was money he needed. Oh, and he hadn't told his wife. It was money he couldn't afford to lose.

Another investor who contacted me lost £250,000 on one share and £300,000 on another.

I feel it is pretty hard for us to be honest when it comes to how much we're putting in. I suspect most put too much into the markets. Have a really good look at your accounts now. Have you got too much in?

Over the years I have never added anything new into my accounts except for the annual £20,000 ISA allowance.

Now I could do this easily. But I'm not going to. I am not even slightly tempted.

Right now I have nearly £2m sitting in cash in national savings. (Partly from a house sale.) You might think I would be putting that money in. No. It stays in cash – and national savings is 100% protected money. Maybe I'll buy some property with it.

That money I consider my nest egg for what's left of my life. No way would I consider putting *any* of it in the markets.

There's no need, I am very comfortable, why take the risk?

Consider your total pot of free money. How much of that should be in the market? 20–25% perhaps? If you have £100,000 sitting there, how's about £25,000? You could lose most of that and still be fine. But half of it? Not sure?

Of course, age is a big consideration. Say you're 25 with no commitments. Well then, OK, you can take bigger risks and put more money in.

But in your 30s and 40s with kids? Be really careful, says this boring old fart.

I try and keep money that's in my ISAs in there. Spread betting gains, though? I tend to bank those and keep the winnings in cash.

If I started finding I was losing spread betting, I'd pull out and wouldn't add any new money.

Lessons learned

- Take a good look. Has greed made you put too much into the markets? Or maybe you have a gambling mentality? Or maybe it's just happened accidentally over time?
- Be realistic. If you can see you have too much at risk, cut.
- You'll feel a lot better!

Be a small-cap dummy

Obviously when you're about to buy something, you want to buy at a great time. You really want the share to rise as soon as possible afterwards. And the last thing you need is for a share to start slumping soon after a buy.

If that happens you have problems, especially if it's a small cap and you paid a bit of a spread. You might already be down 3–4% on the spread. If the share suddenly heads down a few more per cent just because a couple of sells came through, your stop-loss could be hit and in just a day you may already be a loser.

Market makers control most small cap shares.

How do we know if it is likely they are about to move a share price up or down?

Level 2 helps. As said, this isn't something I find I can cover in a book; it's simply way too hard unless you can demo it live, which I do at seminars. But there's a simple trick to try and work out if a small cap share price is about to head higher, or perhaps tumble.

Be a dummy and try a dummy order!

That means you're putting in a buy order on your platform of choice to get a 15-second quote.

What signs are you looking for that the share is about to go up and perhaps the market makers are short of stock?

The best sign of the lot is if you put in a buy order for the market size (usually around £2,000–£5,000 worth of shares in a small company) and a quote does not come up. It says the shares can't be dealt. That's a very good sign: the market makers don't want to sell you shares.

In that case, and if you really like the company and actually want all those shares, you could try a limit order 1 or 2p higher than the current price offered, or be really old-fashioned and call your broker and ask what they can get you.

What's a bad sign?

You ask for a large number of shares, and guess what, no problem with getting them, perhaps even at a discount!

That's not good: the market makers want to dump a load of shares on you. Most likely they are going down.

The price you are offered will give some insight as well. Let's say a small cap is 400–410. You put in a dummy buy and you are offered 404, a 6p discount. Not good! The market maker is keen to offload.

Remember: *they are the enemy!* If they are offering you a massive discount off the quoted price, beware enemies giving gifts.

However, say you put in an order for market size, you get a quote and you are offered a worse price – say, 412p. Take it! The price is almost certainly about to rise.

More information can be gleaned from a pretend sell. If you put in a dummy order and you can easily sell tons of them, then don't! The market maker wants to buy the shares from you – don't do it.

Some brokers let you pretend sell shares you don't even own... check to see if your broker does it. Then you can pretend sell different amounts. See how many shares the market makers are willing to buy from you.

If you can't sell that many, then it could be a good time to actually sell them and take some profits – in this case the shares are likely to go down.

Lessons learned

- The crux of it is: don't do what a market maker wants you to do.
- If shares are hard to buy, then buy them!
- If shares are hard to sell, sell them!
- The easier it is to buy and sell lots of shares, the more of a warning sign it is.
- I am talking about market-maker-only small caps here. This doesn't work on bigger companies, like those listed on the FTSE 250 and above.

Buy lower PEs and low PEGs

This is about as technical as I get. When analysts and writers start to drone on about PEGs, PEs, cash flow, MACDs and the like, I start to snore too.

But stay with me – looking at PEs and PEGs is relatively straightforward.

I look at these measures to try and help determine the cheapness or not of a company.

> I feel if the PE seems reasonably low (but not too low) plus the PEG is low, there is a better chance I'm getting a bit of value.

Checking the PE

There are many PEs quoted for companies. I like to stick with one. That way I'm comparing like with like. I use Stockopedia's **forward PE**. This is shown as PE(F) or PE Ratio (f) on a quote page:

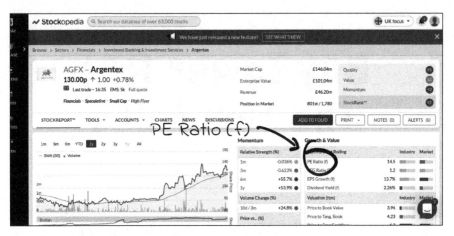

A quote page on Stockopedia

Anyway if you must bore me, Burns, what is the PE(F) ratio all about anyhow?

Stockopedia explains it well, which is rather handy for me as I can just paste its explanation – like so:

"A high PE ratio means that investors are paying more for each unit of Earnings, so the stock is more expensive compared to one with a lower PE ratio. The PE ratio can be seen as being expressed in years, in the sense that it shows the number of years of earnings which would be required to pay back the purchase price, ignoring inflation.

"Investors have a tendency to overreact, becoming enamoured with glamour stocks (pushing their PE too high) while becoming disenchanted with value stocks (pushing their PE too low). Research has shown that low PE ratio stocks tend to outperform high PE stocks in the long run. On the other hand, there are many investors who believe that you should 'pay up for quality' in the same way people pay for jewellery – the best growth stocks therefore rarely trade for cheap PE multiples."

What sort of number am I after?

I like between 8 and 18. Any lower might be a concern. If a stock looks too cheap it may be something is not right, for example debt could be mega.

If the PE is way high, the share is probably expected to have massive growth – and if that growth stalls even a little, the share price can get hammered. It could also just be in a bit of a bubble.

I've been getting quite a few bids for stocks I own recently. I noticed that bids tend to come in when the share is around the 12–16 PE mark. The acquisition price often then takes them to 20–25.

Now just because a PE is in a sweet spot does not necessarily mean it's a buy. You have to do loads of research. Perhaps a share has a PE of 7 and you think 'Hmmm, nice and low.' Then you discover that its profits were good but it is in a sector the market doesn't like right now, so it could go lower. Or maybe – that old classic – it's got a debt problem.

To buy a company quoted at over 20, for me it would have to have fantastic growth prospects. That means looking closely at the PEG.

Checking the PEG

Handily yet again Stockopedia comes to my rescue with an explanation for what a PEG is (I feel very worthy here, I could have pretended I wrote the next bit when I didn't. Well done me.):

> "The PEG is a valuation metric used to measure the trade-off between a stock's price, its earning, and the expected growth of the company. It was popularised by Peter Lynch and Jim Slater. In general, the lower the PEG, the better the value, because the investor would be paying less for each unit of earnings growth.

> "A PEG ratio of 1 is supposed to indicate that the stock is fairly priced. A ratio between 0.5 and less than 1 is considered

good, meaning the stock may be undervalued given its growth profile. A ratio less than 0.5 is considered to be excellent."

Got that? Under 1 is good, and the further under 1 the better.

I have come across some shares with a PEG of 5 or more which does put me off.

I'm not that bothered if it is, say, 1.5 or 2. But a big figure… well, maybe more research is needed to find out the reason why.

My tick boxes

When looking at a quote, my PE or PEG tick boxes are:

- PE in mid teens or less

- PEG of under 1

- Plus a dividend of 2.5% or more (better if it's 4 or 5% if possible).

When I see these three boxes ticked I'll embark on some detailed research. However, if I'm seeing a PE of, say, 28 with a PEG of 3 and no dividend I start to frown and think 'probably best left alone'.

As I write, electric car maker **Tesla** has a PE of 60 and a PEG of 1.8 and no dividend. I'll leave that to the speculators.

At the same time, online shopping behemoth **Amazon** has a whopping PE of over 100, and a PEG of 8.2. Well, yes, maybe the only company left in the world *will* be Amazon when it takes over everyone else. But with figures like that, any disappointments and the price will be *hammered*.

A company I bought while writing this was **ME Group**, which has popped up in a couple of strategies. A PE of 10.5, PEG of 0.9 and a dividend of 6.5%. Those are the sorts of figures that get me interested.

I must remind you: markets aren't easy and nice figures don't necessarily mean profits every time. But if you avoid higher ratios you'll also keep from buying shares that are really risky and could end up bringing down your portfolio.

If you can find a company with a lower PE, low PEG and a decent dividend, you could be buying something with some upside to come.

Lessons learned

- A PE between 8–18 is a sweet spot in my experience. Any lower and a company is too cheap, probably for a reason (e.g. huge debt). Higher and massive growth is expected: if that doesn't materialise on the scale expected, the price will be hit.

- PEG measures the trade off between a stock's price, earnings and expected growth – anything under 1 is good. I tolerate 1.5 or 2 as well. Anything higher... nah.

- I also like a dividend of 2.5%+ alongside these. Reassures me that the figures really mean what they say.

Find the right sector – but be watchful

You can sometimes use common sense to find the right sector to invest in at the right time. Similarly, it's possible to avoid (or short) sectors that are in the doldrums. Or indeed realise the mood music is changing in a particular area.

How?

This is where it's worth keeping your eye on events affecting certain sectors. I often find it's a small news article somewhere like *The Times* that helps.

When you have a bit of time, read through the business pages.

Sometimes it becomes fairly obvious. I used to be heavily into gambling companies because in the USA the powers that be were starting to legalise it. Companies were excited about potential growth in the States, so I bought in happily and made some nice profit. There were also a few bids in the sector.

But then came news of a gambling commission enquiry into the industry. The government was interested in trying to stop people gambling and getting into bad debt because of it. Various barriers arose, and it looked like regulation would make it a lot harder for companies to make profits.

That is when I got out.

But – things *can* swing back in a sector's favour.

In this case, perhaps the regulations won't be as onerous as expected. Money could then pile back into gambling companies and thoughts may again turn to expansion in the States. The sector could then roar back into favour. For me, it is worth keeping tabs on.

The war in Ukraine and some tensions around the world caused the defence sector to suddenly shine in 2022. Shares in defence companies began to rise as governments considered extra spending on defence, and I bought in.

A sign that a sector is going well is when you start to see bids come in for companies in said sector. In defence, a big green flag was a bid for **Ultra Electronics** (nice, as I held some).

Potentially this could lead to other bids in the sector and again push up prices.

When to exit?

Well, in this particular case, hopefully tensions ease in Ukraine and elsewhere, less money is then made available for defence spending, and it is time to quit.

Covid of course changed many sectors for the better and worse. Everyone wanted to do up their homes while stuck there so the DIY sector went manic, and I doubled on Kingfisher, the owner of B&Q, as covered elsewhere in this book. Building companies also benefitted, as did quite a few in the drugs sector.

On the other side, restaurant and retail sectors suffered, meaning that shorts in those paid off.

Once events change, you must change tack.

For example, online clothing companies boomed for some time in the pandemic as the young happily bought cheap clothes over the internet. Shares like Boohoo and ASOS soared, as did all shares in the online clothing sector.

But then things changed. Inflation appeared, shipping costs went through the roof. Also youngsters became more conscious that throwaway fashion was damaging to the environment, so buying cheap clothes online became less appealing.

It became fairly obvious it was time to bank profits and go short as the sector tanked. Both Boohoo and ASOS suffered badly and I made a bundle on a Boohoo short.

Have a good look at your portfolio and the various sectors you are in. Are they in vogue? Are they starting to go down? Could there be a problem with a sector? Is there anything there in the wrong sector? If so, get rid.

Then have a good read and think. What sector is likely to be the next in favour and which out of favour? It just takes a bit of detective work, reading and common sense.

Whatever you do, don't stick stubbornly to shares that are in sectors that are out of favour.

Lessons learned

- It's surprisingly possible to call which sectors are moving in and out of favour by keeping your eyes open.
- Use this to pick companies to investigate further (as longs or shorts).
- Watch the sector closely once you're trading companies in it – things can change quickly.

Play the Christmas rally (spread betting)

I am sure some of you reading this will have already tried playing the Christmas rally – the end-of-year uptick in the FTSE 100 that happens most years. Generally, it's pretty hard to lose money giving it a try (though there are a few key things to get right).

Is it really possible for a strategy this simple to work so routinely?

Well, yes, on the whole, subject to you being very strong and understanding if it doesn't pay off you have worked out the max you can lose – and cut your losses pronto.

But isn't the Santa rally thing a myth – just a story papers/clickbait sites use to fill some space?

Definitely not a myth.

Going back over the years, the FTSE 100 nearly always rises, sometimes quite a lot, in the latter part of December (sometimes carrying on into the next year).

Why?

No one really knows and it doesn't much matter.

Some say it's pushed up so fund managers can claim a better performance, some think people feel happier/more optimistic around Christmas. My view is that people seem to be generally drunk and buy, buy, buy before photocopying their bum at the office party.

Anyway, who cares why? It (mainly) just does go up.

But when exactly do you pull the trigger?

A bit later than you might think.

The stats people reckon the FTSE rises generally on the last ten trading days of the year (exclude weekends and bank holidays). That tends to suggest buying around 10–15 December. You could sell on New Year's Eve, though often it carries on a bit, so you might want to sell in early Jan.

This chapter is about how to do it through spread bets. (Spread betting is a UK thing, but you can do similar trades in other countries using different instruments, perhaps an ETF like in the next chapter.) And as a spread bet we're looking at how many *points* things will move – which translates into how much money we can make, depending on what we stake per point.

Over the years, I've usually found there's between 300 and 400 points available.

Very roughly here's what the last few years could have brought. (This is approximate, and assumes you bought around mid-December and sold at year-end or just after.)

2022	7300–7600 (300 points but it carried on into the New Year for another 200)
2021	7200–7500 (300 points)
2020	6500–6800 (300 points)
2019	7200–7600 (400 points)
2018	About even (0 points, poss −200)
2017	7500–7700 (200 points)
2016	6900–7200 (300 points)

2018 was a difficult one – it was very volatile and most likely you'd have lost (or just about broken even).

Buying pounds per point – say, £10 a point – most years a profit of £3,000 should have been reasonably easy. If you really went for it at, say, £50 a point, then we're looking at £15,000.

I think my best was £25,000. I played 2018 badly and I vaguely remember losing something like £4,000.

Your stake really depends on how big your pot is and how much you are prepared to lose should it be the year it all goes horribly wrong.

The good news is: if you used a guaranteed stop-loss you'll always know your max loss.

When it comes to stops, this cannot be overstated: **Remember that the FTSE is highly volatile.** You HAVE to use a very wide stop, or your trade will be closed out despite the overall movement ultimately going in your favour.

An example. The FTSE is 7000. You place £10 a point at 7000. Where should the stop be? Well, I think *at least 300 points away*, as you don't want to be spiked out. There's no point in setting it 50 or 100 or 150 away. The FTSE can quickly move that much – then move back – and where would that leave you?

If you use a guaranteed stop, worst case you lose £3,000. (300 points times your tenner.)

Let's say it's working out and by Christmas Day the FTSE is 7200. Well, you could now move the stop to breakeven at 7000. On paper, you're up £2,000.

It's now New Year's Eve and the FTSE is 7300. You've made £3,000. You could either bank the profit, or if you feel the rally could continue into the New Year you might move your stop up to nearer the current price, say, 7150. Now, if worse comes to worst, you'll still make £1,500 even if the FTSE tumbles!

By doing this, you're taking a gamble for more profits. Say we're now into January and the rally carries on. We are now at 7500; you can of course move the stop up *again*, this time nearer the price – say, 7,400.

At some point you'll get closed out for a lovely profit.

Lessons learned

- Work out how much you're prepared to lose and set your stop there.
- But ensure the stop is a decent way off.
- Gradually raise the stop up if it goes your way.
- Don't bet too high in case it's the year it doesn't work.

If you are unsure of how to stake, please see the latest edition of *The Naked Trader's Guide to Spread Betting*, which includes more technicalities.

I've tended to use www.spreadco.com/nakedtrader for the Santa rally, as it only has an 0.8-point spread (most others seem to have 1-point spread), though obviously please check this is still the case as things can change.

Play the Christmas rally (without spread betting)

We've discussed playing the Christmas rally by spread betting – but what if you don't trust spread betting and want to stay away from it? Or what if you don't have spread betting in your country?

There is a relatively straightforward way of playing the Santa rally in your normal account using an ETF. (If you're in the UK you can absolutely do this in your ISA.)

How does it work?

As with spread betting this rally, we assume that the FTSE will hopefully go up by 300–400 points. Unlike with spread betting, we're not betting per point rise in the FTSE. We're buying an ETF called **3UKL**.

This is the **WisdomTree FTSE 100 3× ETF.** You'll find it easily enough by putting in the code 3UKL on your platform of choice. Plug it into a real-time monitor and you can see it moving up and down.

An ETF is a fund that you can trade like a share. It stands for exchange-traded fund, but you probably knew that.

The idea behind this ETF is that if the FTSE 100 goes up, this ETF goes up in a magnified away – around three times as much.

Let's say you buy this when the FTSE is at 7000 and the rally takes it to 7400, which is roughly 6%. On a spread bet you'd make 400 times your stake. With the ETF you'd pick up roughly 18%. Not too shabby for a few days.

To carry on with this example:

You buy the ETF just like a share. At FTSE 7000 the ETF trades at 299.5–300p. You buy 3,000 shares, staking £9,000. Costs are tiny – whatever your broker charges you for a standard share buy, and there isn't any stamp duty.

After a 6% FTSE rise, the ETF should now trade 18% higher. Your £9,000 stake is now worth around £10,620. A profit of £1,620.

The ETF is calculated daily, meaning you may not get the full 3×, but it should be close over a smallish timescale.

Now, what happens if the rally doesn't come to pass this year?

Like the spread bet, you can set a stop. Let's say you set a stop 10% away at 270p. Worse comes to worst, you'll lose £900 or so.

As with the spread bet, should the rally go your way you can raise the stop to the breakeven level and maybe into profit should it go well. If the rally carries on into the New Year you could hold further, tightening the stop as you go – till eventually it closes out into profit.

There are no daily or any other costs to holding the ETF, unlike the spread bet which will cost you a bit daily.

You may feel worried about taking on a strategy like this. Anything new or you haven't tried before in the market is always a bit scary. You may wonder: *Can I lose my whole stake in this, or worse – even more than I put in?*

No, not at all. You've got to think of this idea as being the same as buying a share. Except in this case the share will do exactly what the FTSE 100 does, magnified by three.

The magnification is really what gives this strategy a good chance of bringing home profits if you don't want to get into spread betting.

By the way, some of you could do both. I do! That is, you can do the spread bet outlined in the previous strategy *and* buy the ETF in your ISA too. This way you get a bump in both your accounts.

With all strategies you've got to figure: *What are my chances of winning?* I'd say really good, probably 80%+ with this one.

And with the ETF, there's really limited downside assuming you use a stop.

Lessons learned

- If you can't use spread betting, you can still trade the FTSE 100 and benefit from the Santa rally in your ISA – use the 3UKL ETF.

- Make sure you use stops to limit your downside. This year may be the year Santa doesn't come!

Use spread betting like an ISA

If you're reading this in the UK I assume you've probably looked at spread betting, maybe put on some trades, maybe lost your money. (If you're not in the UK you can probably skip this chapter... It's only a short one!)

Possibly you are using it sensibly as part of a tax-free strategy – and in that case, hats off to you.

It really is possible! Many dismiss spread betting as gambling and never try it. Well, it *is* called spread BETTING I suppose. And you don't want to bet, you want to invest.

However, it is perfectly possible – and indeed very useful as a full-time trader – to use spread betting like an investor. To treat it like an ISA. Here's how.

Let's say you have £150,000 to invest. You've been trading for three years and have got £60,000 of that into an ISA tax-free (3× the annual £20k max contribution).

That's great... but what about the rest of the money?

If you make any profits over a set limit (£6,000 in 2023–24, £3,000 thereafter), by trading in a normal (non-ISA) account, the mafia... I mean the *government*... is going to ask you to hand over some of your profits in capital gains tax.

(Strange how, if you lose, they don't have to send YOU money isn't it?)

That's where spread betting comes in. It can be a kind of ISA for you.

But it's not at all the same, surely?

You're wrong: it can be. Almost identical. Here's the thing: apart from the staking, there is very little difference between spread betting or investing in an ISA.

OK, with spread betting you don't own the shares. The firm does. But you get all the benefits in exactly the same way. You get the dividends, exactly as you would in an ISA – indeed paid more quickly. (You get the dividend in cash on ex-dividend day rather than waiting the usual six weeks for it to appear in your ISA.) If there is a rights issue, you're entitled to them.

There is literally no difference except... the staking. But this is really easy to wrap your head around when you realise that 1,000 shares is the same as £10 a point, 5,000 shares the same as £50, and so on.

I teach students at my seminars that if they ever get confused and want to buy 1,000 shares in something at, say, £2 a share – simply tap 2,000 into the spread bet account buy box then remove two zeroes. That's all you have to do every time – just remove two zeroes. £20 is the same as 2,000 shares.

Once you buy the 2,000 shares those shares are in effect yours – with all the benefits.

When it comes to costs, you pay a little extra on the spread when you buy or sell (the firm's profit) but then no commission or stamp duty. And if you do a daily bet (DFB), it might cost you around 15p a day to hold a couple of grands worth of shares. Or, you could go for a quarterly trade, and hold for a long time before any extra costs.

Delve into my spread betting book for more info on this, but just assume holding a share long term as a spread bet costs a bit extra over time, but not *that* much – and it is a small cost to pay considering you have no tax costs.

Spread betting is perfect for range trading (see **Trade the range** strategy). You could hold a range trade for four weeks. You have paid no commission or duty and just a bit of an extra spread. Nice work!

Another benefit with your **spreadISA** (as I like to call it) is more accurate stop-losses. Your stops are *much* more likely to be executed correctly at spread betting firms. With a standard ISA, brokers can be very slow and you can get slippage. Less so with spread bets.

There's also the ability to go short on shares – which isn't possible in your ISA. And, again, it's still tax-free! (You don't have to place shorts, of course, if you're not comfortable with it. It's just an extra option.)

Lastly, there is another benefit which spread bet firms offer… but I don't believe you should use. That is 'margin'. In other words, if you buy a share – say £2,000 worth – you may only need to have £500 in your account. Which means if you stuck £20k into a spread betting account you might actually be able to buy £30k worth or more of shares.

Don't!

If you put £20k or whatever in, only buy up to £20k worth of shares. Don't be tempted to use the leverage at all. Not even a small bit. Trading with money that's not yours changes *everything*, and can lead to big problems.

Always think of your pounds per point as amounts of shares. In other words, you bought £20 a point in Barclays? That is 2,000 shares.

Now, there are downsides if you have a certain mentality. You have to be able to consider this as just another ISA – and use it just as you would your standard ISA. There are lots of traps for those who approach spread betting any other way.

People sometimes also worry too much about the additional small costs if you hold something for months. But it doesn't matter. The costs aren't much – just remember how much profit you're making on the trade.

> It's incredibly easy to overtrade in a spread betting account, to buy riskier shares, to overdo it generally. They're set up to facilitate lots of punts and using tons of margin – but that WILL NOT make you rich as a trader.

If you find you're acting differently in your spread betting account, putting on lots of trades and going wild, you must stop and close it. It's brought out the gambling side in you and that's dangerous for your trading – indeed fatal.

Stop immediately, quit the account, never go back.

You'll know in your heart if this is you.

You might be amazed in the end at how well a spread betting account can work for you. Remember, used the right way, it is just another ISA – and it means you can use a whole lot more money to work for you tax-free.

Lessons learned

- Most people lose at spread betting because they use it like a gambling account. But there's nothing to stop you treating it like an ISA. It's, in fact, an excellent idea if you've used up your annual ISA allowance, or if you want the flexibility of shorting.

- The only major difference is the staking. Remember that 1,000 shares is the same as £10 a point, 5,000 shares the same as £50, and so on.

- Never use the margin. Free money is, of course, a trap.

Treat trading as a business

I meet a lot of would-be investors who say things like "This is going to be a fun hobby for me."

Nope.

It doesn't matter whether you have a fiver or 500 grand, **trading is a business.**

If you treat it like a hobby you are doomed.

This is your money

It isn't just a bit of fun. This is your money we're talking about. I bet you had to work hard for it. The moment you think it's a hobby you are less likely to make anything.

Because you just won't make a proper plan, you won't cut losses when they happen, and you'll make every mistake there is – because who cares, it is just a hobby.

If you're in any business and you're the owner you'll always be considering costs, scrutinising bills, looking carefully at what you're spending your money on. Which is exactly what you need as a trader.

A share is your stock. You're buying stock to turn a profit. If you were a restaurant owner you'd be looking at the right food to buy to make good money on it.

If you treat the restaurant more like a hobby, that's no good. You'd buy any old stuff for fun and see what happens.

I ran a café many years ago, and traded shares from the back office. I was always getting visits from people trying to sell me stuff, from meat and veg and coffee to office chairs and fridges. All kinds of things. My job was to buy decent quality items at the right price for my business.

It's exactly the same with shares. Just like a business you have to learn to buy decent quality – at the right price!

Every buying or selling decision you make has to be thought through properly for your shares business.

The buck stops here

Which brings me to share 'tips'. People would often rather buy shares because someone they don't know tipped it on the internet!

This is like me pondering which smoothie tastes the best at a good price and some bloke I don't know comes up to me in my old café and says "Yeah, buy that one."

Am I really going to do that?

As a trader YOU are in effect a fund manager. Make sure it's you that makes the business decision to buy something, not some bloke off the internet or down the pub.

As a fund manager running a business you ought to be on top of all your stock – in this case your shares. You should always know where you are, what price you paid, what price you're looking to sell.

You should be keeping an eye on the news – anything that might change how the market perceives the shares in your portfolio.

One of the hardest things I remember at the café was having to fire someone. They had to be fired because they were underperforming.

Frankly it's a lot easier cutting an underperforming share than an underperforming member of staff!

Especially in one case when a member of staff had a blackbelt in karate. I was ready to dive under the desk or make a run to the exit to ensure a foot wasn't planted in the knacker area.

Indeed, think how much easier it really is to run a portfolio as a business instead of a normal business. It's one of the reasons trading is great.

But always remember: *this is a business.*

It isn't a hobby or a social activity. Don't be tempted by too many Twitter and internet social hookups and meetings or else you'll be doomed.

Be strong with your business, and execute your business plan ruthlessly.

Lessons learned

- Treat trading like a business. It's the only way to be disciplined and rigorous.

- Keep on top of your 'stock' – the shares you are buying. You have to buy decent quality at a decent price. And you have to know what you're prepared to sell them for.

- I'm not saying you can't enjoy yourself. But making money is the point – and you can use those profits to have fun. Don't trade for fun as an end in itself. This is business!

Get with the screens

I've always found screening for shares the best way to find new shares to look at.

Why?

Well, looking for that share that hopefully will make you at least 20% is a bit like finding a needle in a haystack to quote a wretched old cliché. But if you use the right screening tools, the search can become a little easier – a bit like lowering a large magnet over all that hay.

Using screens is a big help on the psychological front too. If you rely on getting shares from magazines, tipsters, forums and suchlike you are opening yourself up to confirmation bias and the influence of others.

For example, if you buy a share because a character on a forum bought it, you are now hanging on their every word. If you are tempted to sell at a loss you probably won't because they'll say "buy more" etc.

If you get your shares from screens, you're cutting out all that noise and concentrating on cold hard figures.

That's difficult in a way. We're a pack animal and want someone else to lead us (into temptation). But it's vital to get away from that. Only read forums and the like minimally – and get your shares from screens!

If you find a share yourself and build your own plan you're more likely to make money because you're more likely to cut the loss should it end up a stinker.

Which screens?

I already looked at value and momentum together. Here are some more screening ideas that I find very useful. Most of them cost a little bit to use, but you can often get free trials. And unfortunately you do have to spend a little bit of money to run a trading business. Think of it as start-up costs. At least you're not buying sacks of coffee.

Stockopedia screens I use

After looking at Stockopedia's quality/momentum screen idea earlier in the book, let's look at some others.

Jegadeesh and Titman

Over on Stockopedia, under **Guru Screens** click **Momentum Investing** then **Price Momentum Screen**.

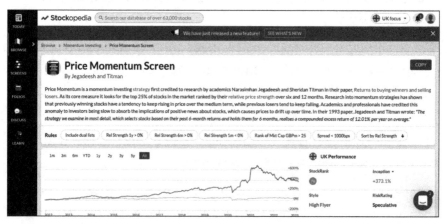

Stockopedia's Price Momentum Screen

This is the **Jegadeesh and Titman** screen – sounds like an MOR rock group. *"Now ladies and gentlemen, a big hand for... Jegadeesh and Titman!"*

This screen looks for the top 25% of stocks in the market ranked by relative price strength. I've found some decent ideas from this in the past. In effect it's finding **the strongest rising shares**. (Obviously, ignore any penny share stuff that comes up.)

Your time is valuable. Go through the ones with the highest stockrank first.

Make sure you're not buying what looks like a decent share but which momentum has simply taken way too high for now. And, of course, do your research as you would in the normal way. But this screen may surface something moving upwards with purpose – and which has much further to go.

Top StockRanks

Top StockRanks is another screen that can bring up some candidates for trades. This one is based on shares that Stockopedia's system rates the highest for quality, value and momentum.

A reminder: of course, *this doesn't necessarily mean these shares are fantastic.* We are looking for the golden needle.

Stockopedia's Top StockRanks

Super Stocks

Another one that can throw up good 'uns is found by clicking **StockRank styles** and **Super Stocks**. That should bring up some decent ones to begin research on.

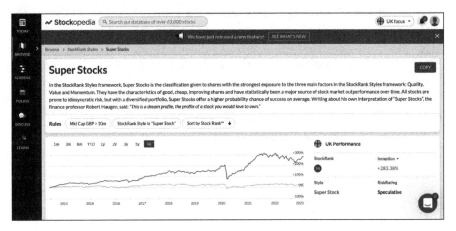

Stockopedia's Super Stocks

There are a shed load of screens on Stockopedia – take your time to find the ones that suit your style/brain.

And remember: simply because you're trying to find shares yourself rather relying on people you don't know (and who are probably mad addicted gamblers), you are already more likely to find success.

ADVFN screens I use

ADVFN.com has some interesting screens that I like using.

You'll need to click **Toplists** then **Premium Toplists** on their homepage to get to these.

They charge for these, but not a lot at the time of writing. If you call them and mention my name they'll probably give you a nice discount. Though if you've bought this in the bargain bucket at the bookstore in 2031 they may say "Robbie who?"

Breakouts

Their Breakouts screen is a decent list. Click the 'Period' box and set it at 52 weeks. Ignore the 'Variance' and 'Date' columns.

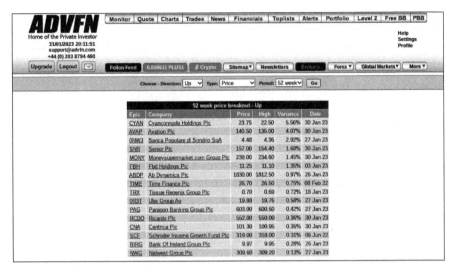

ADVFN's 52-week breakouts

Just take a few of these shares out at random (unless you know them). These are all shares that are breaking out of a previous range, which can be a decent pointer that something might be happening with them.

At the very least you're picking up on movements which could be signalling something good to come.

However, you *can* get false breakouts. In other words, the share pops up on this list – but then reverses and heads back down. Keep a very firm eye on things in case this happens. You may want to exit fast.

The best time to scan for 52-week breakouts is actually after a few days of the general market being down. Or even a few weeks. Because shares breaking out during a downturn is a very good sign indeed.

This might also help in spotting sectors moving up during downturns.

You can click on the dropdown list and you'll find 'Volume'. This picks up on shares dealing in heavier volume than normal. It's possible to pick up on some big buying, which could be a pointer.

If you're into shorting, click the first dropdown menu and then click **Down**. Check the mid dropdown menu says 'Price'.

This screen picks up on shares that are having a bad time, breaking down through previous strong support. This could signal bad times ahead – great for lists of shorts.

Constant Gainers

Moving on to some others, I quite like the **Constant Gainers** screen. This picks up on shares that might be moving up under the radar. It can find shares which have been moving slowly up in small increments.

Look for shares that have gained for a few days; start with the ones that have gained for most days in a row then work back.

You could find some shares moving gradually up which could signify some buying going on in the background.

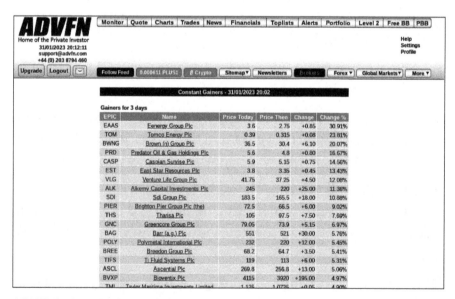

ADVFN's Constant Gainers

Constant Fallers

If looking for shorts, click on **Constant Fallers**. This screen looks for shares where the price has been very gradually falling day to day. This one might be worth a look in case one of your shares is on it!

If it is – and has been on there for a few days – you may want to re-consider your position.

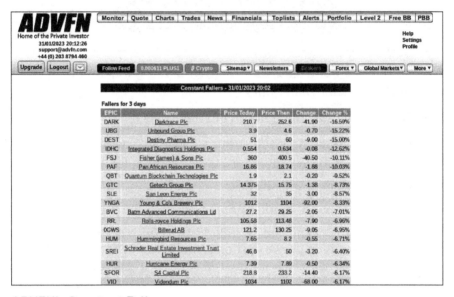

ADVFN's Constant Fallers

Percentage Losers and Gainers

There are some useful free screens on ADVFN too. You'll find **Percentage Losers** and **Percentage Gainers,** for instance. Click on these just after market open to check nothing you own is involved in the losers league table. Be happy if you're involved in a gainer.

It could be you have to move fast to get involved with a bigger percentage gainer – fast research could be needed. Be careful of jumping in too fast.

With percentage losers, it is tempting to say "Oooh that one is down 30% it will recover later today, I'm in for a quick bounce."

But it could just as easily head further south. As always, be wary of making too quick decisions.

Perhaps generally, you ought to consider screening outside market hours – at weekends, for instance. Give yourself plenty of time to research and relax. Remember, you're looking for that golden share that looks great out of a load of ones which really don't.

Lessons learned

- Screens are a great way to find shares. They strip out the human element (and confirmation bias that comes with it), relying on cold, hard figures.

- They cost a little, but you can get free trials.

- Screens surface *potential* trades – you still need to do your usual research on a company. Most companies on a screen aren't going to make the cut.

- Use screens out of market hours to reduce the pressure. Take your time. We're trying to find something special. This is a shortcut – not an instant list of immediately attractive trades.

Buy the up/ average up

We discussed recovery plays earlier, and how wary you have to be buying shares that have gone down a lot.

I generally prefer buying strongly rising shares and averaging up in them. In other words, buying more as they rise. That's because something good must be happening with the share – it's going up for a reason. Perhaps its story is changing, or its markets are in a good space.

> It's crazy to think that investors are happier buying shares that have gone *down* because there are problems with the business rather than shares going *up* because things are going well.

Recovery plays are loved by investors, as they assume they're buying a bargain. By contrast, buying shares that have risen for a bit isn't that popular. The thought is, "It's already gone up, I missed the boat."

A good example of this is **H&T**, the pawnbroker. You could have picked this up on a breakout screen at 375–400p. And you could have bought on what looked like a big high around there – but *it kept on going*, with another 15% rise even from the highs.

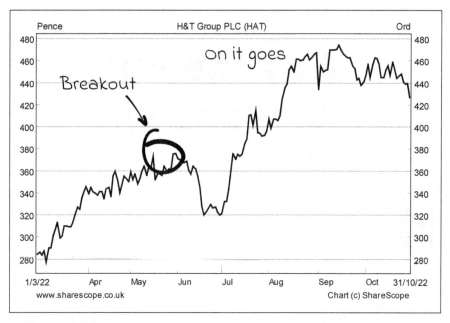

H&T – pawn stars

This is because markets are often slow to catch onto rising shares. They can carry on rising for a lot longer than you'd imagine.

Make sure, of course, that the company you buy looks like good value even after rises.

Often I find that once I've taken a position in a good 'un, which gradually keeps rising, I'll continue buying – averaging up. Most people hate that. The mindset is: "I bought it lower, I'm not buying any more now it's higher." Well, why not, if it still looks good – and people are now noticing it (as reflected in the price)?

For example, I started buying defence company **Ultra Electronics** in June 2021 at 2068p. It just carried on going up, as its sector came in vogue. I bought more at 2350p and more at 2550p, even though I was already up 500 points since my first buy. The market will carry on re-rating shares where the story is changing. Eventually it got bid for at 3500.

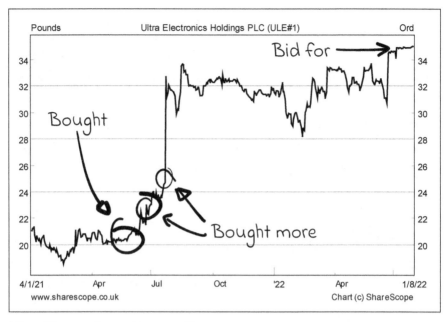

Ultra Electronics – ultra excellent

My latest buy on the up as I write this is **Ricardo**. I bought some at 392p in July 2022, even though it had already risen from 320p. It carried on rising from there, and I averaged up at 415p then at 420p. It continued rising through 450.

After the rise through 450p, I set the stop in the 392p position to 400p and the 415/420 to 420 at breakeven.

Should it continue rising, I can move up the stops.

Of course, averaging up like most strategies isn't going to work every time. For example, I bought a share called **Gattaca** at 150p, averaged up at 200p, but then got caught out by a warning. Though stops got me out at an overall profit, I'd been too complacent with the average up and hadn't noticed a couple of warning signs.

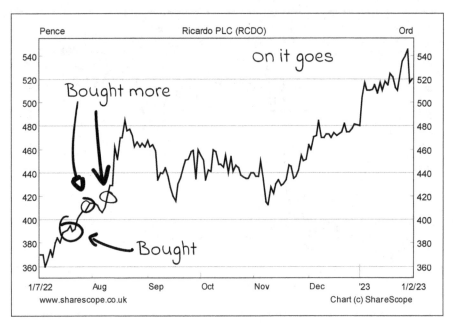

Ricardo – profit secured

If you're averaging up, one useful approach is to buy the new shares in a different account as I did with Ricardo above. I bought some shares at 392p, and bought more at 415p in a different account, then treated the positions separately. You can have different stops on the two positions. You might end up taking a loss on the average up, but keep the original position.

Don't just buy something because it's rising. You need to do the usual proper research, and decide whether it's really worth it or it's just rising on momentum with nothing much behind it.

Perhaps add in the *Dragons' Den* strategy to a fast riser. Would Peter Jones still be interested at the raised valuation?

Lessons learned

- It's better to buy shares that are going up – including ones you've already bought. Clearly something is going right, and now people are noticing. That's good!

- This is more reliable than trying to pick companies about to reverse direction – though psychologically tougher for some reason.

- Maybe buy your average-up trades in a separate account so you can see how they perform and set different stops for them than your original trades.

Recovery plays the right way

Investors love recovery plays. Given a ton of these lose money, that isn't great.

Why do we love recovery plays?

Something about collapsed prices makes us irrational, while simultaneously feeling totally rational. A share has tanked a lot because it has had a lot of problems. Instead of nodding at this state of affairs and finding other companies to investigate, we think: "Oooh, this share was 400p now it's only 80p. I must be getting a *bargain*. I'm going to buy it. It's not crap – it's a *recovery play*."

We say to ourselves: "Look how far it could go back up! If it even goes back up to just *half* of what it was I'm going to double!"

It is very tempting – too tempting for some. I have met traders who will only ever try and buy recovery plays. They think that's what investing is.

But…

It is, I am afraid, all too possible that a beaten-up share isn't a 'recovery play' but a continued stinker that will carry on stinking – and going down.

Most shares fall for a reason. Many collapse for several.

One bloke who came to a seminar couldn't help himself and would only buy shares that had gone down a lot. He bought major stakes in shares like the AA (400p to 35p) and Carpetright (700p to 10p).

"They've got to go back up," he said – and kept saying. And he blamed everyone but himself for his problems. He eventually concluded it was all Donald Trump's fault!

I *do* buy the occasional recovery play. On the whole, I'm more interested in buying shares that carry on going up – but the odd recovery play can pay off. I do emphasise 'odd'. It's amazing how companies whose share prices are tanking can simply carry on going down… and sometimes go bust.

What should you look for in a recovery play that might actually be worth buying?

- Firstly, you need to carefully consider what it was that pushed down your potential recovery play in the first place. Have these problems been resolved? Are they truly likely to be? If they're external factors, are they still in force – or likely to come back?

- Secondly, how are the finances? Has debt ballooned? Will they need to raise more money at a lower share price?

Let's look at some examples. *(Yes, let's Robbie – enough waffle.)*

The share price of cinema company **Cineworld** kept falling throughout 2020–22. Well, kind of. There were times the price motored up as traders considered it a recovery play. Many thought: "People are going back to the cinema after Covid, the new James Bond movie is out and look at those buckets of popcorn at £10!"

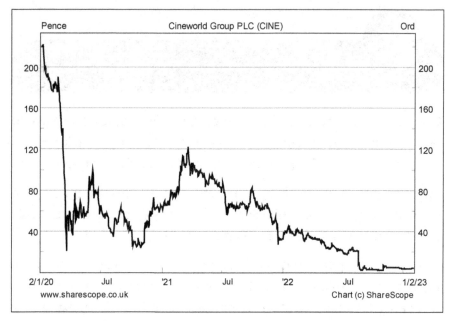

Pence   Cineworld Group PLC (CINE)   Ord

www.sharescope.co.uk   Chart (c) ShareScope

Cineworld – crockbuster

But I felt it was quite straightforward that this was NOT a recovery play and the price was likely to fall further.

Why, oh mystic oracle?

The debt.

While Cineworld was forecast to go back into a small profit in 2023, net debt was – get this – nearly £9 BILLION. Yes, I did say £9 BILLION!

It was fairly obvious that either the company was going to go bust or it would have to raise massive sums of money, which inevitably meant diluting shareholders and further large share price falls.

Another point to consider was the threat of streaming services. With the easy (and ever-increasing) availability of premium movie and TV content online, it remained likely that fewer people over time would visit the cinema.

One of the main things to always check if you're about to buy a recovery play is *what's the debt?* Could it go bust? Does it need more money?

If you have Stockopedia, check the **Bankruptcy** meter. Beware if it shows 'Distress'.

What to look for in a recovery play that might actually be tempting?

I want something where the story is changing for the better and there is either low debt or some cash. One such trade for me was **QinetiQ**, a defence company. Shares had fallen from 400p to 250p, hit by concerns there would be less spending on defence.

However, it really did begin to look a bargain at 250p. Governments were announcing renewed spending on defence, the company began to announce new contracts... and best of all, it had a massive cash pile.

A recovery play that ticked all the up boxes for me – and I felt I could buy with confidence.

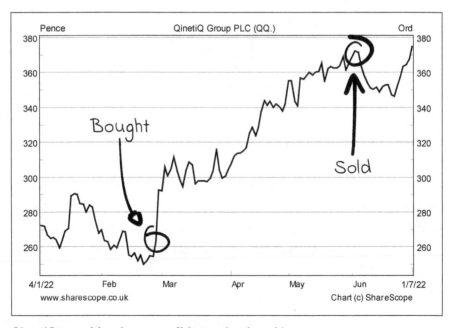

QinetiQ – cashing in on confidence (and cash)

Another example of a recovery play not to buy? **Purplebricks,** the online estate agency. This company fell from 400p to 30p and never looked tempting even when directors bought shares.

Why?

Because there seemed little change in the story. House sellers just never seemed to grow keener on using the firm. They still wanted to use bricks-and-mortar agents. The Stockopedia bankruptcy needle remained firmly pointed at 'Distress'.

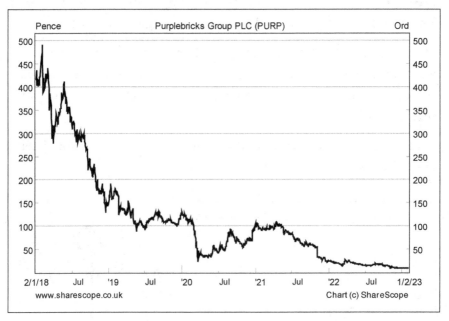

Purplebricks – bricking it

To go for a recovery play, then, you need to know firmly why a recovery could actually be on the cards – backed with either a very low debt or net cash. Don't fool yourself into buying a play that's heavy in debt and no story change just because the price has tanked 85%!

Lessons learned

- Shares usually fall for a reason. But recovery plays are possible if problems have been resolved.

- Check they really have been – and check the finances are OK too.

- Don't be swept up by false recoveries. Enthusiasm cannot overcome things like huge debt, even if prices might rise briefly.

- Find stories that are changing for the better – and where there's low debt and some cash.

Be logical, captain

In a few of *The Naked Trader* books I suggest modelling yourself on Mr Spock off Star Trek (and not Jonesy from *Dad's Army*).

In other words, be logical, cool, calm and collected.

But something logical Mr Spock would definitely consider is: *what catalyst is there in a company you're about to buy that could propel it a lot higher?*

It mystifies me when I see investors buying into companies that just don't appear to have anything that could lift their shares price a lot higher over, say, the next year.

Investors don't think about it. They just go: "Oh, look how far this share price has gone down, must be time to buy."

But WHY?

You must have a strong *logical* reason to buy a share. If you don't, why buy it – even if it's gone down a lot recently?

The reason must be one that could push it up. If you can't think of any really good reason for why it might march up at some point soon, why the hell are you buying?

There are some real small investor favourites that have no obvious catalyst at all. I've mentioned some of them already in the book:

- **Cineworld.** More debt than a small country, and fewer and fewer people are going to the cinema.

- **Purplebricks.** People like traditional estate agents and showed no desire to use an online-only one, even in a pandemic. Who wants to sell their most valuable asset online?

- **Card Factory.** We all know people don't buy as many cards anymore. There's now plenty of online competition. And the items it sells are all pretty small beer. What's the point?

- **Superdry.** Youngsters don't want to wear it. When you see middle-aged people wearing a fashion brand, you know it's in trouble.

- **Smiths News.** It distributes newspapers. Fewer and fewer people are reading papers. It's a slowly dying business, and forecasts are for slow profit declines. A chap at a recent seminar just didn't get it. "But it's only trading on a PE of 3." True, but there is a reason.

What would Mr Spock look at instead?

Probably shares with catalysts like these:

- **BAE Systems.** Sadly, more wars in the world means more government spending on defence. And defence companies have been bidding for each other. Plenty of chances for rises here.

- **Bloomsbury.** People are buying more and more books – publishers are in great demand. Mr Spock would look out for bids. And what's the downside? Kids aren't going to stop reading *Harry Potter*.

- **Spire Healthcare.** Mr Spock knows with NHS waiting lists people are self-funding their operations more and more. Plenty of catalyst for upside.

Think hard before you press the buy button. Do the Mr Spock test. Have you identified a coldly logical catalyst? You need a very good reason to buy. What is it? What is coming up that could really, truly propel a share price *upwards*?

If you can imagine Mr Spock's right eyebrow rising in incredulity upon learning of your trade, it's time for you to boldly go and buy something else.

Lessons learned

- You need a strong logical reason for a share to move up before you buy it.
- Make sure you really have identified a cold, hard reason for such a move.
- Wishful thinking is common in this area – and useless.

Trading in a pension

I get asked quite a lot about SIPPs. These are **self-invested personal pensions.** You can have one at most places you have an ISA. They're simply pensions made up of shares or funds you buy and sell yourself. (If you're outside the UK, check the pensions rules and tax wrappers in your country – there's almost certainly something similar.)

Are they worth having? And, if so, how do you run yours compared to an ISA?

I reckon it's definitely worth having a SIPP and running it alongside your ISA (and spreadISA).

It isn't as good as an ISA in my opinion. There are a lot of rules. But if you have a company scheme or a pension sitting there not doing much, why not transfer it to a SIPP and run it yourself?

I got the £32,000 transferred from my last job 22 years ago into a SIPP, and over those years have taken it to over £500,000 with no new money. I reckon if I'd left it to the fund managers it would be, what, maybe £70,000 now if I was lucky?

It's a no-brainer if you enjoy investing to transfer any existing schemes into a SIPP unless you have one of the older 'final salary schemes' which were very generous.

You get tax relief on contributions. Every time you put money in the UK government grits its teeth and adds some on top (always check online for the exact latest rules).

Downside? You can only take out 25% tax-free (after age 55 at the moment), and after that you pay tax at whatever the current income tax rates are.

Personally, then, I trade in my ISAs and spread betting accounts – and run my SIPP as a pension plan.

What's the best strategy to run your SIPP with?

This really depends on your age/circumstances and pot size compared to what you've got in your trading accounts and general money pot. Overall, I'd look at running your SIPP as if you were a fairly cautious fund manager.

After all, it is supposed to be your pension. It's there to pay out in your dotage, so hopefully you can enjoy your retirement without having to worry about money.

I would suggest a few rules for a pension strategy that are on the cautious side. Why not? You can take more risks in your other accounts. Consider your pension a nice comfortable pair of slippers.

My pension rules

The first rule on any pension holding? **A decent dividend.** Only allow stocks in there that pay out at least 3%, preferably nearer 4 or 5%. With this rule, income should be very nice, especially if you have a big pension pot transferred from a company scheme. At least then, even if sometimes shares weaken, there's the income.

You may not even want or need to withdraw anything from your pension till you're, say, 75. Therefore you could have years to let it grow, even if you're already in an older age group.

Now consider what kind of shares you want to have in there. Let's say you have £250,000 in there. I'd suggest £200,000 of it should be in **larger shares** with good dividends. Look for **shares which tend to grow their profits** over time. Perhaps some **giants of the**

FTSE 100, some **decent 250 co's**, maybe even delve into a couple of **US bluechips**.

I'd then put the rest in **small caps** – and maybe a tiny amount in a couple of punts, for a bit of fun. However, even with small caps, keep to the dividend payout rule. No dividend? No buy.

You should consider some of your buys to be longer term, maybe something like a five-year time horizon.

Do you need stops? Well, yes, in case of a major market downturn, but I'd set them a fair distance away. Consider the SIPP as something not to tinker with too much. Perhaps even think of yourself as a longer-term fund manager – buy and sell only infrequently. Maybe just look at your SIPP once a month and consider a change or two then.

Have a few bigger holdings in there – shares with the highest dividends and in the most defensive industries. Your SIPP is your solid, defensive, boring fund! You shouldn't really have to worry too much about the ups and downs, there are years ahead.

What about additions to the pot?

I wouldn't add any further to a SIPP unless you've already topped up your ISA allowance for the tax year. If you have extra money at that point that you really don't need – as opposed to funds you actually want to trade with (which can go in a spreadISA) – then consider putting some more in.

But always remember: once in, it's a pain to take money out, especially if you've already banked your 25% tax-free lump sum later in life. You'll have to pay tax to get at it.

It's also definitely not worth breaching whatever the maximum amount you're allowed to have in before the tax rate goes even higher. If you are lucky to have the max amount (currently around £1m) it simply isn't worth adding any more.

Good luck with your SIPP: remember, take it easy and relax with it. Slippers are supposed to be comfy.

Lessons learned

- Prioritise your non-pension tax-free trading accounts first. It's easier to access the money. But it's not a bad idea to transfer an old pension into a SIPP (or your own country's version of that) and trade it yourself too.

- Unless you have a very generous final salary scheme, or anything like that, in which case don't mess – and if at all uncertain, get advice!

- Fill your pension with big, solid, boring companies paying big, solid, enjoyable dividends.

- Buy for a five-year horizon or longer, and don't tinker.

- This should be the trading equivalent of warm slippers. Over time, it should do nicely – and certainly better than the fund managers!

Have a gamble!

Gambling? What! What kind of strategy is this, Burns?

I thought you were all safety this, dividend that, stop-loss this, bitcoin is for losers that. Be careful, boring, blah blah blah.

Yes, all that is true. But I reckon there is a gambler in me that needs some satisfaction. And my bet is, many of you reading this are part gambler too!

Anyone that gets into share trading *has* to realise there is a risk taker in them somewhere. If we didn't have one, we'd stick the money in the bank, or be in funds, or premium bonds.

I used to be a pro gambler on the horses in the 90s, so I definitely have a gambling streak! My best win was £2,000 on an 8–1 shot. I spent the next year picking up cash on my bike from 25 different bookies across London.

The urge to sometimes throw caution, stop-losses and common sense to the wind is definitely there for me. Probably for you too. But I have ways of stopping that. One of these is little sports gambles for fun on football and the horses. Just small stakes.

The other is to do with shares. If you feel you always end up gambling on risky shares too much, here is a strategy to get out of it!

Simply set up a totally separate shares account – with a different broker to whoever you use for your ISA or other shares accounts.

Put a very small amount of your total share trading pot in there. How about 5%? Tops 8%. Say you have £200,000. Stick £10,000 of it away in this separate account. (If you have less than £20,000 to trade with, this strategy probably isn't worth it – you won't have enough to play with.)

And what do you do with this account? GAMBLE!

Yes, go CRAZY! Buy any old crap with it. Small oil companies, cryptocurrency, currencies, punts, tips from bulletin boards, jam-tomorrow stories.

Don't bother with stop-losses, discipline, or anything. Go for shares with wide spreads, whatever the hell you like! Go wild. You're a gambler in this account. This account doesn't need to be run as a business. It's for FUN!

Would you believe it, this strategy works!

I've mentioned this strategy over the years to people who were struggling and found they couldn't help gambling money away in their main accounts. And it *works*! I have had many grateful emails from investors telling me this really does put their gambling to bed.

With their other accounts, they can be serious, businesslike and manage their money properly. Their gambling account really does satisfy the gambling urge.

There are a few rules about this, though:

- After you put in your fun money do NOT add any more in for a year if the balance goes down. You'll just have to gamble with less money!

- You can allow yourself to top up a little a year later as long as your main business is going well. But only ever at a max 8% of your total shares fund.

- If you win, keep the money in the gambling account and enjoy bigger sums to bet with.

- Don't use a spread betting account to do this on margin. It defeats the object!

> If you find you keep adding money into this account because of heavy losses then this is a sign you really are a reckless gambler at heart – and you ought to consider whether you should be trading at all. It is worth contacting Gamblers Anonymous; there is always help.

Do NOT buy any sensible shares. Stick to potentially terrible penny punts and jam tomorrow companies! Put small money into lots of silly trades. One or two may succeed, giving you the thrill you seek.

You may think this strategy is a bit of fun on my part. Not so! It really does work. If you are a boring old git who would never consider a gamble (lucky you!), then of course there is no need for you to have a side gambling account.

Some of you won't be gamblers – or will have mastered the urge so completely that this has no appeal. If so, that's very good. *Don't start doing it!*

This is only for those of you who know you have a gambling side in you that is likely to come out in trading. You will know it if you do!

You do? Get the side account set up (subject to my rules).

You don't? No need, and disregard this idea completely!

Lessons learned

- Many traders have a little gambler in them. After all, we're risk takers.

- To avoid that contaminating the business of trading, open a separate account with strict limits on the total pot – and absolutely no limits on anything else.

- Go crazy. Gamble as much as you like.

- But never add more, and never use margin.

- Don't use this a prompt to start gambling if you don't have such urges.

- If this doesn't work, then stop! Rethink trading altogether if necessary.

Shun the publicity-hungry

Traders are often keen to buy shares in companies which put themselves about. By that, I mean firms whose head honchoes and big cheeses appear in hotels trying to drum up publicity or interest.

Or companies that try and attract small investors to buy their shares in any way they can. Investor days, for example. Or by getting involved with as many tipsters, commentators, etc. as possible.

Just this very morning I got an email from a company – which I won't name for obvious reasons (let's just say it was a small one). This was the chief executive – mailing me! He said he thought I might be interested in an article about his company.

I'm a polite chap and a people pleaser – I hate confrontation. Instead of saying: "This is a huge red flag, the only thing I'd think of doing right now is shorting your shares," I said something like: "Thanks for thinking of me and good luck."

He replied: "Just wanted to increase the profile of my company, we are based in the middle of nowhere – lol."

It was the "lol" bit that got me. I mean, if you are a CEO you need to maintain a *bit* of gravitas!

I looked the company up on Stockopedia. I just knew it was going to be labelled a 'sucker stock'. And sure enough, it was. There seemed little chance of making any profits and it looked terribly high risk.

The bottom line is: if your company is going well and has great prospects, the market already knows, or will soon enough. You really don't need to go out there and spread the word. Fund managers and investors will find you from the numbers – don't worry about that!

I think companies that put themselves about are often doing so out of desperation. They want to get the share price up. If they can just attract some buyers to get things moving, they may then be able to raise fresh money at a better share price. Or just keep the wolf from the door for now.

But it's not just desperation. It hurts the bottom line too. They have to pay to exhibit at shows. And all that time on the road is a distraction – shouldn't they be at their desks working on winning contracts?

I was suckered a few times when I started trading, by CEOs with shiny shoes and great patter. The first company I bought into after visiting it went bust six months later.

What other warning signs are there to look for?

Too many stock market announcements. Announcements that are insignificant such as 'Investor presentation' or 'We won a contract for £100'.

Of course, not *every* company is out there trying to deceive. If you are at a presentation, you might even be able to sift out the good from the bad. Here are a few things to watch out for – or to put to them in person if there's Q&A time:

- How much money have you got?

- What is the net debt picture now – and likely to be in six months' time?

- What real profit are you making (*not* EBITA)?

- What is the profit forecast for next year?

- If you're not likely to make a profit, and you don't have much cash, is there going to be a fundraising?

Make sure you get good answers before you part with your money. Don't fall for a story. They're easy to spin. New products and markets always sound good – but where are the buyers right now, and the profits? If they duck profit and debt questions in particular, be wary.

And in general, I think you should be suspicious if a company is appearing everywhere, inviting investors to visit, always at events. There is probably something not right. You're better off buying companies which just get on with it, publish four statements a year and don't need to generate PR. Or, more accurately, BS.

Lessons learned

- Companies that put themselves about can be oddly appealing, like they're being candid and doing you a favour. And Q&As, investor days, etc. can feel like real research.

- But results speak for themselves, and traders are always trying to find good companies. If a firm has to go to such efforts to make themselves known, how good are they really?

- If you do attend these kinds of events, grill the people mercilessly. Maybe – just maybe – you'll find something worthwhile if the answers are good.

- But investor outreach is less useful for investors than a company simply putting its head down and making dosh for its owners (investors).

Have a mix of longs and shorts

This strategy is not going to interest a number of you. I get it – some people just won't go short. But doesn't it make sense to try to back decent companies on the way up, and bet on companies doing badly to go down?

We've discussed shorting already. In this strategy I want to focus on how a mix of these with longs will make you more money longer term, except for periods when the whole market moves in one big direction (like at the start of Covid).

Most traders including myself have a long bias. We want to buy shares that are going up. But what about the bad ones? Why not make money from those too?

In my spreadISA account (i.e. my spread betting account which I use as if it's an ISA, as discussed earlier) I have a mix. I am happy to have some shares sitting in the account that I think are going to rise, and some I believe are likely to fall.

Take the two biggest winners in my spread bet account at the moment. They are both making me a profit of about £40,000 as I write this. One is a long or a buy, and one is a short or a sell:

- I have a win on **Telecom Plus**, which I bought because energy markets were changing in its favour.

- And I have another big win on **Aston Martin**, because it has gone down a ton. I've been betting on it to fall because of its massive debt and poor profit potential.

The two positions sit happily in the same account even though they're making money for very different reasons.

Why is this approach effective?

Firstly, it makes the most of your time. It means when you find an over-priced stinker, your research hasn't necessarily been wasted. And it means you can make money when markets, or sectors, are moving in all sorts of different directions. You don't need to wait for sunshine to make hay.

Secondly, it helps with your mindset. It gives you a fuller flavour of what's going on, as well as how companies move – and are affected by everything from fundamentals to news cycles. It makes you feel less helpless, blown along by general market trends and unable to act, or stuck because you can't find a company that will go up.

It also teaches you first-hand what it takes for a company to do well – and how it can all go wrong without that. (You can and will learn that from buying companies that don't go up, of course – but it's better and more rewarding to learn it from shorting companies that tank too.)

After all, surely we just want to make money in the markets – so why not have a mix of long and short?

Another example of big winners in my spreadISA being balanced between longs and shorts:

- A short I put on **Wise** because of a crazy high PE is really paying off for me; its shares have halved.

- Meanwhile a long in **Indivior**, a drugs company that could rise once it gets a US listing, is going up strongly.

I like having this balance.

Won't it get terribly confusing?

Not really. In most accounts it is easy to keep track of both your longs and shorts. Shorts will generally have a minus sign next to them, and be in red. Looking down an account, I can easily see what I've backed to go up, and what down.

Depending on how your brain works, it's worth pondering how best to monitor both longs and shorts. I keep them in the same monitor, but I know some prefer to have separate ones. One monitor can track your longs, and one your shorts quite easily if you find having them all in one list confusing.

Is there anything to be wary of in pursuing this beautiful blend?

I do think you should be careful about mixing longs and shorts in the same sector. This can be pointless; your short and long can cancel each other out.

For instance, I see little point in having a short in, say, **Ramsdens** as well as a long in **H&T**. They are both pawnbrokers doing the same thing. They will probably roughly both go down or up depending on circumstances. Yes, individual company financials matter – but so does the sector they're in. If business in one area is bad, it's usually bad for all the companies within it (though there are always exceptions).

Each long and short should have an appropriate stop. With shorts, this needs to be *above* the current price (as you lose money should the share be rising).

I am not a subscriber to one idea some traders have. That is, to be long *and* short of the same share at the same time. The idea is you have a long-term position in a share but short term it is going down. You hold one position for the long term while making money shorting it briefly. This one does my head in – but good luck to you if you can achieve it.

By mixing longs and shorts, you can make money both ways – and basically run your own hedge fund. You flash git!

Lessons learned

- A mix of shorts and longs makes for a productive portfolio.

- If you find an over-priced stinker, your research isn't necessarily wasted – perhaps it's a profitable short waiting to happen.

- Shorts and longs blended together means you can make money when markets move in different directions.

- This also gives you a better flavour of everything going on across the market, and how firms are affected by good and bad news.

- Don't bother having a short and long in the same sector: they will often cancel each other out.

Three strikes and you're out

There's one thing I always tell traders to do. It's possibly the hardest thing for them to do – but reaps the most overall rewards.

And what's that?

Simple: **if you have lost money on a share three times, do not get involved with it again for at least three months, preferably six.**

And stop watching shares that you've lost money on.

There's nothing worse for any of us than spending time thinking about (or looking at) some flipping annoying share that we always seem to lose money on. Time and time again.

You end up holding and holding, buying more, convincing yourself it will come back... till eventually you bite the bullet and sell and take that loss.

And then it begins again... unless you do this one simple thing. Get rid, and vow never to even look at it till a set period of time has passed.

While it is good to take a loss, it's also to important to cut ties with a losing share – at least for a while. This strategy may not only save you money, but also save your soul! All the time you would have spent watching a company, agonising about when to buy it back – well, you can do something much more interesting (and profitable) with that time instead.

It is perhaps similar to ending a relationship. Much as you loved the other person, there is no point in seeing her or him again for a long time. Or else it's back to heartbreak.

Let's take the example of a share, **Boohoo**. Thousands of traders kept buying this as it tanked from 400p to 50p. Some did decide to take losses on it before it really hit rock bottom.

Let's say you bought some at 400p, eventually you decided you couldn't take the pain any longer and sold at 250p. But then you bought some more at 240p! You couldn't resist! It looked so cheap and that bulletin board guru was telling you it was a great time to buy.

Oh no. It went down to 200p and you sold out again.

Then it went to 180p! So cheap! Must buy, must buy.

Oh no. Again. Down to 150p. That is it, I am out forever!

But you're not. You want revenge, you're going to keep watching Boohoo, every day, every hour for another chance. The money you lost was money lent.

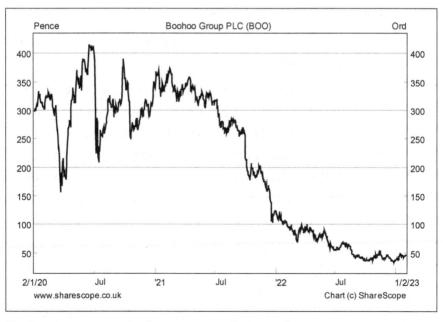

Boohoo – never was a share more aptly named

No. Don't do this.

At this point you operate the three-strikes-and-you're-out strategy.

You have made your final loss. Now you take Boohoo off your monitor for at least 3–6 months. Do not let temptation get the better of you.

Six months later, take a look. It's 50p. Well, that saved you a bundle!

An example from my own trading. I bought a share called **Ince**, thinking it looked cheap. I paid 76p for it, and set a stop of 68p. But, whoops, there was a profits warning. I was stopped out at 52p, taking a stinging and unexpected loss.

But hang on, it looked cheap. I bought more at 48p. Stopped at 44p.

Right. One last go (stupidly). Bought at 42p, stopped at 38p.

I'd lost nearly £2,000 overall on these three buys. Time for three strikes and you are out!

I immediately took the share off my screen. Never looked at it, never read any of its statements. Six months later, I had a look. Hell's bells. It was 5p! Three strikes and you're out saved me.

Here's a message from someone who bought Rolls-Royce shares, who I shared this strategy with:

> "Thank goodness. I bought Rolls-Royce shares three times and every time it ended up a big loser. I am glad to say today I have taken a loss for the last time. I have stopped watching it and I feel so much happier. It's like something that was making me sad and annoyed every day has gone from my life and I can move on. I'm on holiday soon and I am sure I'll now enjoy it more."

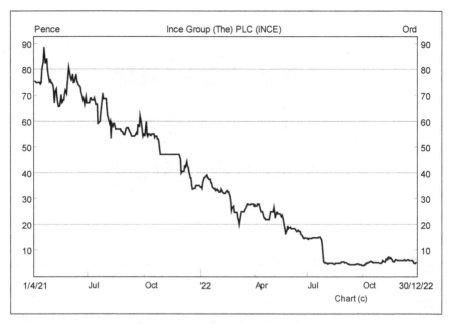

Ince – three times and I was out (thankfully)

With this strategy I'd also suggest using ever tighter stops for the second and third time you buy a share that keeps falling. Have a look through your trades now. Is there anything you've taken losses on three times now? You know what to do.

The market really is telling you: get out, stay out!

Lessons learned

- Lost money on a share three times? Put it out of your mind (and all accounts) for at least three months – ideally six.
- Cutting ties will save you money and sanity.
- Use tighter stops on your second and third attempts to trade a company.

Buy boring (but not too boring)

I f there's one thing traders hate, it's a boring-looking company.

What kind of boring?

Maybe a firm that makes screws and sockets. Or a company with no chance of finding oil in swamp land in Africa. Or a business totally uninterested in discovering gold in a river in Iraq.

Lots of traders hate that sort of thing.

They generally want excitement! They need it. There is little point suggesting they buy something with a dull story where profits tediously increase every year. *Yawn!*

Yet boring can, with patience, provide some distinctly less-than-dull trading profits.

For instance, you can't get more boring than providing energy services to social housing. But what if the company involved – **Sureserve** – just keeps on seeing rising profits every year... for *years*?

Sure, what it does is dull (though rather important). But its dull services are needed more and more. Plus it has built up a cash pile which could be used for acquisitions.

The share prices of companies like these tend to stay put for long periods, but from time to time will jump when more profits are revealed. You can tuck these bores into an ISA, sit there and wait. (Unless question marks suddenly appear, or a stop gets hit.)

True, these aren't the kind of shares that double overnight. But you really do need some slow Steady Eddies in a portfolio.

You could argue that pawnbroking is a fairly boring business. But it's the type of consistent business that should always make a decent profit – and it's (usually) unlikely you'd get a massive drop in shares. Pawnbroker shares like **Ramsdens** and **H&T** tend to be ignored. Too unexciting. But sometimes these boring businesses get an upgrade during an economic cycle – H&T rose 50% over a few months in 2022.

One day you'll notice that boring share you bought for the ISA and go: hang on, that's gone up quite a bit, and I got some dividends too!

However, be careful you're not buying a boring business that is also gradually declining.

For example, **Smiths News** looked a solid boring business, and it was paying a great dividend. It delivers newspapers and magazines to wholesalers. An ideal boring ISA tuckaway, surely?

Ah, but look more carefully. Its business is not just boring – it's old-fashioned, and dying. Younger generations are ditching papers and reading online. I don't think it will necessarily crash. A steady share price decline is more likely, unless it changes tack.

Facilities by ADF looked pretty boring when it floated. A dull business that was easy to understand. It provides the trucks and equipment needed for outdoor location shooting for movies and TV shows. Yes, good, steady and boring – but given the huge amount of new content being produced for the growing world of streaming, it is likely to also be kept busy.

Considering it also has a good slice of the market and could use cash to buy up competitors, it's the kind of boring share that could sit in an ISA and one day get upgraded as results surprise.

In the end, I think it's quite important to have the right kind of boring companies in an ISA portfolio that can be left for a while. When you come across one of these while scanning for shares, perhaps think 'Yes, great, boring' rather than 'Boo, rubbish, boring'.

Tedium isn't enough. You also want generally rising profits, lack of debt and ideally some cash. And do a sense check on whether the company is in a declining area. If all looks the right kind of boring, though, it's time to get excited!

Lessons learned

- Exciting-sounding companies don't necessarily make exciting profits. Often the reality is the reverse.

- Dull but important services and products, however, can prove very exciting over time.

- Stuff your portfolio with a few of these Steady Eddies and you'll be smiling.

- Not all boring companies are great, of course. But where 'yawn, boring,' is often used as a first filter to dismiss companies in research, you want to switch to 'oh, boring – this could be good'... and go from there.

Keep a balanced portfolio

E very portfolio should have a carefully curated mix of different types of shares. Not only companies in different sectors, but a selection of smaller and larger shares. The bigger the spread you have – the more varied the mix – the less likely you are to suffer heavy losses.

If your portfolio is too heavily weighted towards one sector then you could be in for trouble should said sector come under fire. For example, you could have a load of oil shares. You may get lucky and they all go up... but what if sentiment turns? All your shares will fall.

Also, consider how much you have in each share. Is your portfolio too heavily weighted towards just one or two firms? Have a balanced approach. And remember that bigger holdings are safer when in larger, liquid companies. They're risky in small, illiquid ones because if things go wrong then it can be hard to sell. And you don't want shares in a portfolio that are hard to sell.

My ideal mix would be some small shares, some larger shares, a real mix of businesses, all weighted roughly the same.

I thought the best way to explain would be to go through one of my current ISAs and share what's in it.

Company name	What it does	Size
Argentex	FX company	Mid cap
BAE Systems	Defence	Large cap
Begbies Traynor	Insolvency practitioner	Small cap
Bloomsbury	Publisher	Small cap
BP	Oil	Large cap
Computacenter	IT	Large cap
Concurrent	Computer solutions	Small cap
Facilities by ADF	Film/TV facilities	Small cap
GB Group	ID Technology	Mid cap
H&T	Pawnbroker	Small cap
iEnergizer	Software	Mid cap
Indivior	Drugs	Large cap
K3 Capital	Insolvency	Small cap
ME Group	Photo booths/laundries	Small cap
Morgan Sindall	Construction	Mid cap
Next Fifteen	PR	Mid cap
Redrow	Property	Large cap
RBG Group	Legal	Small cap
Ricardo	New energy	Mid cap
Team 17	Computer games	Mid cap
Telecom Plus	Utilities	Large cap
Science	Science services	Small cap
Sureserve	Support services	Small cap
Totally	Medical services	Small cap
Watches of Switzerland	Retail	Large cap

As you can see, there is a massive variety of different companies, a bit of nearly everything. There's 25 companies, and I have between

£5,000 and £10,000 in each. A bit more in the mid and larger and a bit less in the small. Also, a wide range of small, medium and larger companies.

The bigger your pot grows, the more companies you'll need in there to keep it balanced and also to ensure you're not heavily weighted towards one or two companies.

And the bigger your pot grows, the more looking after a portfolio will need.

But, of course, it's a business – and as a business grows it does take more time.

> If you haven't had a good look at your portfolio for a bit, it's a good exercise to go through and write down what sector each one is in. You may get a surprise. Have you been buying too much of one sector by mistake? Are you too full of retail shares, or property shares? You may need to slowly take action; perhaps sell down one sector if you are too heavily weighted.

Once you have it nicely balanced, add the discipline of stops and consider selling some of a share you've done well with – especially if, after rises, you've got too much of one.

I think most traders end up weighted too heavily in one sector or with too much in one share.

Think *balanced* – in every way.

Lessons learned

- Portfolios work best when you have a mix of different types of share by sector and size.

- And when your holdings are all a reasonably similar size.

- Periodically go through and make sure you haven't got top-heavy in any one sector or holding. Sell down if you have. It's fine – and wise – to take profits in such a case.

THE
END

My strategies in action

We've talked about a whole load of strategies in this book, so how's about concluding by showing you another one of my portfolios as it stood at the beginning of 2023?

Here's a screenshot of another ISA I have:

Market	Quantity	Avg Price	Book Cost	Sell	Market Value	Profit/Loss	Profit/Lo...
Alliance Pharma PLC	7500	51.0771	£3,830.78	59.40	£4,455.00	£ +624.22	16.29
Alpha Group International PLC	200	809.955	£1,619.91	1770.00	£3,540.00	£ +1,920.09	118.53
Argentex Group PLC	4000	86.58	£3,463.20	121.2	£4,848.00	£ +1,384.80	39.99
Bloomsbury Publishing PLC	1000	331	£3,310.00	447.5	£4,475.00	£ +1,165.00	35.2
Craneware PLC	175	1745.6	£3,054.80	1845.00	£3,228.75	£ +173.95	5.69
D4T4 Solutions PLC	1000	190.572	£1,905.72	238.50	£2,385.00	£ +479.28	25.15
EKF Diagnostics Holdings PLC	15006	44.3609	£6,656.79	48.00	£7,202.88	£ +546.08	8.2
Facilities by Adf PLC	15000	45.7467	£6,862.00	53.00	£7,950.00	£ +1,088.00	15.86
GB Group PLC	1000	215.845	£2,158.45	341.0	£3,410.00	£ +1,251.55	57.98
H&T Group PLC	56	199	£111.44	475.0	£266.00	£ +154.56	138.69
iEnergizer Limited	3000	263.9513	£7,918.54	404.00	£12,120.00	£ +4,201.46	53.06
IQGEO Group PLC	4000	160.1155	£6,404.62	188.50	£7,540.00	£ +1,135.38	17.73
K3 Capital Group PLC	1500	134	£2,010.00	343.00	£5,145.00	£ +3,135.00	155.97
Knights Group Holdings PLC	5000	88.5012	£4,425.06	106.50	£5,325.00	£ +899.94	20.34
LBG Media PLC	5000	64	£3,200.00	104.00	£5,200.00	£ +2,000.00	62.5
ME GROUP	5000	87.4	£4,370.00	114.00	£5,700.00	£ +1,330.00	30.43
MS INTERNATIONAL PLC	1000	457.3	£4,573.00	680.00	£6,800.00	£ +2,227.00	48.7
Next Fifteen Communications ...	250	432.532	£1,081.33	1010.00	£2,525.00	£ +1,443.67	133.51
Oxford Metrics PLC	5000	102	£5,100.00	108.00	£5,400.00	£ +300.00	5.88
Ricardo PLC	2251	399.518	£8,993.15	510.0	£11,480.10	£ +2,486.95	27.65
Solid State PLC	500	687.1	£3,435.50	1410.00	£7,050.00	£ +3,614.50	105.21
Sureserve Group PLC	7500	69.17	£5,187.75	85.00	£6,375.00	£ +1,187.25	22.89
Telecom Plus PLC	450	1218.1756	£5,481.79	2055.0	£9,247.50	£ +3,765.71	68.69
Victorian Plumbing Group PLC	10000	39.188	£3,918.80	92.0	£9,200.00	£ +5,281.20	134.77
Yu Group Plc	1000	380	£3,800.00	555.00	£5,550.00	£ +1,750.00	46.05
			£102,872.63		£146,420.23	£43,547.60	42.33%

Total account value **£151,957** · Open Positions **£146,420** · Profit/Loss **£43,547** · Funds **£5,537** · Available to Deal **£5,537**

Another ISA of mine

This is a newer ISA account. I've had it for about five years. At the time of writing I haven't yet put in the yearly £20k you're allowed to – but will do before the end of the tax year.

Why have more than one ISA?

It might strike you as surplus to requirements, but having ISAs with a few different providers can be handy for a number of reasons:

- If you hold a smaller company and it issues a profit warning, its shares can become *very* hard to sell in any size. Once you sell a small amount with your broker you may find they won't accept another sell for some minutes. But if you hold the same overall amount of shares just spread across two separate brokers, you can sell two lots of shares at the same time – enabling you to get out of the trade more easily.

- Brokers can be different. One might allow direct market access, another won't. One might have particularly good stop-loss options. By having multiple accounts you can gradually discover the strengths and weaknesses of different brokers, and start using different accounts for different trades.

- I also like having an account for longer-term trades.

Anyway, back to this screenshot!

From left to right you can see the quantity of shares held, the average price I paid, what it cost me in total, the current price per share to sell, the market value of my holdings and current profits or losses – though, luckily for me, nothing is losing. And finally the percentage increase or decrease.

Some became long-termers because they kept on rising. Most pay decent dividends. Some I have topsliced previously (banking some profit) if the holdings became top-heavy.

Around £150,000 is divided between 25 positions here, with a rough average of £6,000 per position. This means if anything goes really bad – or even bust – there's no major worry.

You can see I've avoided tricky sectors like commodities and oil, concentrating on shares I think I can place a reasonable valuation on. Sectors are varied – drugs, FX, publishing, tech, defence, green tech, utilities, etc. If one has a major move down, I shouldn't be affected too badly.

I'm happy to sell some of a share rather than all, especially if it gets too big a part of the portfolio. When I sell something – or add the £20k new cash allowed per year – I'll find something else to add.

If there is no cash left and I don't want to replace anything then I will spread bet something instead to remain tax-free.

Of course, by the time you read this some shares have gone and been replaced. The idea here is to provide a snapshot of one of my portfolios in time so you can see my ideas in practice. After a few more years, I expect the portfolio to be totally different!

The whys and wherefores

Some of these shares are already covered in various other parts of the book. But here's a quick summary of my thoughts on each position.

- **Alliance Pharma –** A recent buy based on a recovery-play strategy. A drugs company beaten down by a not-great pandemic. An occasional high risk for me, but at PE of just 7, any good news could see a big upside.

- **Alpha Group –** Has more than doubled and become a long-term ISA hold. Bought on net cash and sector strength strategies.

- **Argentex –** Took advantage of other traders banking profits on a good statement to buy in. Up 44% and potential for longer-term hold.

- **Bloomsbury –** Traded an 'ahead of expectations' statement. Up 45% and wonder if it could be a bid target with its fine fundies.

- **Craneware** – A recentish buy with a sector strategy (the US health industry has been booming).

- **D4T4** – Bought a couple of years ago, I topsliced but held the rest. You'll have to forgive me, I can't remember why I bought it!

- **EKF** – A purchase from a mix of strategies: nice net cash and in a sector that is going places. Potential for longer-term hold.

- **Facilities by ADF** – A mix of a promising sector and a lowish PE. Top of the pops in its industry of providing facilities for film and TV producers.

- **GB Group** – A small rump left in this portfolio for a former high flier. Took profits long ago. Keeping the small bit left here for recovery prospects.

- **H&T** – Only 56 shares left after a botched sale!

- **iEnergizer** – Bought as a potential bid. Has already been bid for once, so hoping for another – which is why I'm holding.

- **IQGeo** – A net-cash play, which delivers geospatial solutions to telecoms – so a bit techy! Highly rated so would come out fast should it dip much.

- **K3 Capital** – Bid target and net cash strategies got me in here. Indeed it has been bid for at 350p, so I'm about to bank the profits. A nice hold which got me 155% profit over a couple of years.

- **Knights Group** – A legal services company which came through a torrid time, a recovery-play idea.

- **LBG Media** – The risky share in this portfolio. Youth publisher on various media platforms. Risky as youths can change what they read/use just like that. Recent buy, up well already, now hope to get a profit.

- **ME Group** – Massive cash pile and a growing new business.

- **MS International** – A massive rise in net cash and a strong outlook got me into this one, then I got a bit lucky as a big contract win was announced. Up 45% in just a couple of weeks.

- **Next Fifteen** – PR outfit, long-term hold.

- **Oxford Metrics** – Net cash strategy and a recent buy. Had sold a big business and now has a massive cash pile. If it could put that cash to some use, it could have big upside.

- **Ricardo** – Green sector (environmental consultant), currently liked by the market. Plan to hold longer term if poss.

- **Solid State** – Held for a couple of years and doubled on it, will keep running profits.

- **Sureserve** – Bought with the boring strategy! A long-term defensive hold.

- **Telecom Plus** – Solid utility with big dividend; long-term hold.

- **Victorian Plumbing** – Trading with the 'ahead of' strategy. Already nearly doubled and could be more to come.

- **Yu Group** – Recent buy also from the 'ahead of' strategy. Looked cheap and despite good rises I am already hoping for more.

The most important lessons

We've covered lots of do's and don'ts in the last couple of hundred pages. I hope the strategies and real-life examples have provided real inspiration, and that these lessons are useful summaries you can refer back to.

As we finish, I'd like to leave you with a summary of the most important lessons. If you forget everything else, remember these:

- Have a plan. Keep records. And use stop-losses, always.

- Be happy with part of a ride. You probably won't sell a share at its peak. That's OK. Forget trying to. You can make millions by enjoying part of the ride.

- Keep your eyes open. Talk to people. Read the news. Be a detective. Attentiveness is often rewarded.

- Statements and results have an impact on companies. Make sure you trade around them mindfully.

- Net cash is always a positive. Net debt is always a danger.

- Opportunity generally knocks in the FTSE 250 and away from the ultra mega global corporates.

- Portfolios should be balanced like a good team. A bit of defence, a bit of attack, a range of different talents.

- Your mindset can hold you back for years. But you can also change it in minutes.

- Changing your mind or your strategy is often vital, and profitable. Never get too invested in getting a particular call right. Be flexible. Be nimble.

- The end of the world is rarely actually the end of the world. You can take action to defend yourself in your trading – and even profit.

- You don't have to enter a trade immediately just because you found a great company. Look at past price movement. Use alerts. Be patient. The right entry will come.

- Avoid groupthink and crowd stupidity. Lots of people are often very loudly wrong together. Even sensible message boards can be overrun with it. Meanwhile the numbers don't lie.

- Companies with a range of income streams offer lower-risk bets.

- Be ruthless in the pursuit of quality companies.

- Treat your trading like a business.

- Avoid anything too clever, anything driven by PR, anything that relies on wishful thinking, and anything that someone else told you was a great idea. Let the numbers talk, trust in simple and logical methods, always cut losses quickly if things go wrong, and keep in the game – you will win over the long run.

Remember: you *can* trade the markets to fund the life you want. My time as a trader is proof. And this book is the map. Enjoy your journey!

Robbie

Appendix

Offers

I am delighted to say I have secured some nice discounts for the platforms I use in my trading. If you're thinking about giving them a go, use the below links to snag a free trial or a decent discount:

- stockopedia.com/nakedtrader (20% off, plus a 14-day free trial)

- sharescope.co.uk/nakedtrader (free month and a free trial)

- ADVFN (email robbiethetrader@aol.com for the latest offer)

- www.research-tree.com/code/nakedtrader (20% off broker notes)

- spreadex.com/nakedtrader (good for spread betting smaller companies)

- spreadco.com/nakedtrader (tight spreads on bigger companies, FTSE 100)

Naked Trader seminars

I hold online seminars a few times a year for beginners and improvers. Spend a day with me and live markets! Email me (robbiethetrader@aol.com) for details or see the latest dates at nakedtrader.co.uk.

Naked Trader retreats

Small groups of traders can also spend three days with me and my wife, a professional trading coach, in Spain. Email me for details on the above address.

Questions about anything?

I am happy to answer questions at robbiethetrader@aol.com

I will usually reply to all emails unless they are along the lines of "You bald tosser". Shorter emails get quicker replies!

Websites

For market commentary, trades and some fun, head to: nakedtrader.co.uk

For trading psychology help, check out: coachingwithelizabeth.co.uk

For free news, see: investegate.co.uk

YOUR TRADING COMPANIONS

Everything you
need to know to
start trading

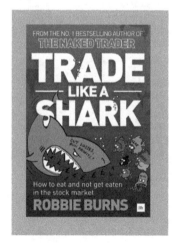

Everything you need
to know about
trading psychology

Everything you need
to know about
spread betting
(UK only)